Privacy and Surveillance

ISSUES

Volume 168

Series Editor

Lisa Firth

Independence

Educational Publishers
Cambridge

First published by Independence
The Studio, High Green
Great Shelford
Cambridge CB22 5EG
England

© Independence 2009

British Library Cataloguing in Publication Data
Privacy and Surveillance – (Issues Series)
I. Privacy, Right of II. Privacy III. Electronic surveillance IV. Firth, Lisa
323.4'48

ISBN 978 1 86168 472 1

Printed in Great Britain
MWL Print Group Ltd

Cover
The illustration on the front cover is by
Angelo Madrid.

CONTENTS

Chapter One: A Surveillance Society?

Chapter Two: Personal Privacy Issues

Useful information for readers

Dear Reader,

Issues: Privacy and Surveillance

With approximately one CCTV camera for every 14 people, the Government's proposed identity card scheme and the introduction of biometric passports, some believe the UK is now one of the most watched societies in Europe. Are these measures necessary in a time when the threat of international terrorism is ever present, or are they an unacceptable infringement on our civil liberties? This book examines the debate surrounding our right to privacy.

The purpose of *Issues*

Privacy and Surveillance is the one hundred and sixty-eighth volume in the **Issues** series. The aim of this series is to offer up-to-date information about important issues in our world. Whether you are a regular reader or new to the series, we do hope you find this book a useful overview of the many and complex issues involved in the topic. This title replaces an older volume in the **Issues** series, Volume 82: **Protecting our Privacy,** which is now out of print.

Titles in the **Issues** series are resource books designed to be of especial use to those undertaking project work or requiring an overview of facts, opinions and information on a particular subject, particularly as a prelude to undertaking their own research.

The information in this book is not from a single author, publication or organisation; the value of this unique series lies in the fact that it presents information from a wide variety of sources, including:
⇨ Government reports and statistics
⇨ Newspaper articles and features
⇨ Information from think-tanks and policy institutes
⇨ Magazine features and surveys
⇨ Website material
⇨ Literature from lobby groups and charitable organisations.*

Critical evaluation

Because the information reprinted here is from a number of different sources, readers should bear in mind the origin of the text and whether the source is likely to have a particular bias or agenda when presenting information (just as they would if undertaking their own research). It is hoped that, as you read about the many aspects of the issues explored in this book, you will critically evaluate the information presented. It is important that you decide whether you are being presented with facts or opinions. Does the writer give a biased or an unbiased report? If an opinion is being expressed, do you agree with the writer?

Privacy and Surveillance offers a useful starting point for those who need convenient access to information about the many issues involved. However, it is only a starting point. Following each article is a URL to the relevant organisation's website, which you may wish to visit for further information.

Kind regards,

Lisa Firth
Editor, **Issues** series

** Please note that Independence Publishers has no political affiliations or opinions on the topics covered in the **Issues** series, and any views quoted in this book are not necessarily those of the publisher or its staff.*

ISSUES TODAY
A RESOURCE FOR KEY STAGE 3

Younger readers can also now benefit from the thorough editorial process which characterises the **Issues** series with the launch of a new range of titles for 11- to 14-year-old students, **Issues Today**. In addition to containing information from a wide range of sources, rewritten with this age group in mind, **Issues Today** titles also feature comprehensive glossaries, an accessible and attractive layout and handy tasks and assignments which can be used in class, for homework or as a revision aid. In addition, these titles are fully photocopiable. For more information, please visit the **Issues Today** section of our website (www.independence. co.uk).

Overview of privacy

Information from Privacy International

Privacy is a fundamental human right. It underpins human dignity and other values such as freedom of association and freedom of speech. It has become one of the most important human rights of the modern age.

Privacy is recognised around the world in diverse regions and cultures. It is protected in the Universal Declaration of Human Rights, the International Covenant on Civil and Political Rights, and in many other international and regional human rights treaties. Nearly every country in the world includes a right of privacy in its constitution. At a minimum, these provisions include rights of inviolability of the home and secrecy of communications. Most recently written constitutions include specific rights to access and control one's personal information. In many of the countries where privacy is not explicitly recognised in the constitution, the courts have found that right in other provisions. In many countries, international agreements that recognise privacy rights such as the International Covenant on Civil and Political Rights or the European Convention on Human Rights have been adopted into law.

Defining privacy

Of all the human rights in the international catalogue, privacy is perhaps the most difficult to define. Definitions of privacy vary widely according to context and environment. In many countries, the concept has been fused with data protection, which interprets privacy in terms of management of personal information.

Outside this rather strict context, privacy protection is frequently seen as a way of drawing the line at how far society can intrude into a person's affairs. The lack of a single definition should not imply that the issue lacks importance. As one writer observed, 'in one sense, all human rights are aspects of the right to privacy'.

Privacy is a fundamental human right

Some viewpoints on privacy

In the 1890s, future United States Supreme Court Justice Louis Brandeis articulated a concept of privacy that urged that it was the individual's 'right to be left alone'. Brandeis argued that privacy was the most cherished of freedoms in a democracy, and he was concerned that it should be reflected in the Constitution.

Robert Ellis Smith, editor of the *Privacy Journal*, defined privacy as 'the desire by each of us for physical space where we can be free of interruption, intrusion, embarrassment, or accountability and the attempt to control the time and manner of disclosures of personal information about ourselves'.

According to Edward Bloustein, privacy is an interest of the human personality. It protects the inviolate personality, the individual's independence, dignity and integrity.

According to Ruth Gavison, there are three elements in privacy: secrecy, anonymity and solitude. It is a state which can be lost, whether through the choice of the person in that state or through the action of another person.

The Calcutt Committee in the United Kingdom said, 'nowhere have we found a wholly satisfactory statutory definition of privacy'. But the committee was satisfied that it would be possible to define it legally and adopted this definition in its first report on privacy:

'The right of the individual to be protected against intrusion into his personal life or affairs, or those of his family, by direct physical means or by publication of information.'

The Preamble to the Australian Privacy Charter provides, 'A free and

democratic society requires respect for the autonomy of individuals, and limits on the power of both state and private organisations to intrude on that autonomy . . . Privacy is a key value which underpins human dignity and other key values such as freedom of association and freedom of speech . . . Privacy is a basic human right and the reasonable expectation of every person.'

Aspects of privacy

Privacy can be divided into the following separate but related concepts:

⇨ Information privacy, which involves the establishment of rules governing the collection and handling of personal data such as credit information, and medical and government records. It is also known as 'data protection';

⇨ Bodily privacy, which concerns the protection of people's physical selves against invasive procedures such as genetic tests, drug testing and cavity searches;

⇨ Privacy of communications, which covers the security and privacy of mail, telephones, e-mail and other forms of communication; and

⇨ Territorial privacy, which concerns the setting of limits on intrusion into the domestic and other environments such as the workplace or public space. This includes searches, video surveillance and ID checks.

Models of privacy protection

There are four major models for privacy protection. Depending on their application, these models can be complementary or contradictory. In most countries reviewed in the survey, several models are used simultaneously. In the countries that protect privacy most effectively, all of the models are used together to ensure privacy protection.

Comprehensive laws

In many countries around the world, there is a general law that governs the collection, use and dissemination of personal information by both the public and private sectors. An oversight body then ensures compliance. This is the preferred model for most countries adopting data protection laws and was adopted

by the European Union to ensure compliance with its data protection regime. A variation of these laws, which is described as a 'co-regulatory model', was adopted in Canada and Australia. Under this approach, industry develops rules for the protection of privacy that are enforced by the industry and overseen by the privacy agency.

Of all the human rights in the international catalogue, privacy is perhaps the most difficult to define

---

Sectoral laws

Some countries, such as the United States, have avoided enacting general data protection rules in favour of specific sectoral laws governing, for example, video rental records and financial privacy. In such cases, enforcement is achieved through a range of mechanisms. A major drawback with this approach is that it requires that new legislation be introduced with each new technology so protections frequently lag behind. The lack of legal protections for individuals' privacy on the Internet in the United States is a striking example of its limitations. There is also the problem of a lack of an oversight agency. In many countries, sectoral laws are used to complement comprehensive legislation by providing more detailed protections for certain categories of information, such as telecommunications, police files or consumer credit records.

Self-regulation

Data protection can also be achieved, at least in theory, through various forms of self-regulation, in which companies and industry bodies establish codes of practice and engage in self-policing. However, in many countries, especially the United States, these efforts have been disappointing, with little evidence that the aims of the codes are regularly fulfilled. Adequacy and enforcement are the major problem with these approaches. Industry codes

in many countries have tended to provide only weak protections and lack enforcement.

Technologies of privacy

With the recent development of commercially available technology-based systems, privacy protection has also moved into the hands of individual users. Users of the Internet and of some physical applications can employ a range of programs and systems that provide varying degrees of privacy and security of communications. These include encryption, anonymous remailers, proxy servers and digital cash. Users should be aware that not all tools effectively protect privacy. Some are poorly designed while others may be designed to facilitate law enforcement access.

The right to privacy

The recognition of privacy is deeply rooted in history. There is recognition of privacy in the Qur'an and in the sayings of Muhammad. The Bible has numerous references to privacy. Jewish law has long recognised the concept of being free from being watched. There were also protections in classical Greece and ancient China.

The right to privacy is set out in the 1948 Universal Declaration of Human Rights

Legal protections have existed in Western countries for hundreds of years. In 1361, the Justices of the Peace Act in England provided for the arrest of peeping toms and eavesdroppers. In 1765, British Lord Camden, striking down a warrant to enter a house and seize papers, wrote, 'We can safely say there is no law in this country to justify the defendants in what they have done; if there was, it would destroy all the comforts of society, for papers are often the dearest property any man can have.' Parliamentarian William Pitt wrote, 'The poorest man may in his cottage bid defiance to all the force of the Crown. It may be frail; its roof may shake; the wind may blow through it; the storms may enter; the rain may enter – but the King of England cannot enter; all his forces dare not cross the threshold of the ruined tenement.'

Various countries developed specific protections for privacy in the centuries that followed. In 1776, the Swedish Parliament enacted the Access to Public Records Act that required that all government-held information be used for legitimate purposes. France prohibited the publication of private facts and set stiff fines for violators in 1858. The Norwegian Criminal Code prohibited the publication of information relating to 'personal or domestic affairs' in 1889.

In 1890, American lawyers Samuel Warren and Louis Brandeis wrote a seminal piece on the right to privacy as a tort action, describing privacy as 'the right to be left alone'. Following the publication, this concept of the privacy tort was gradually picked up across the United States as part of the common law.

The modern privacy benchmark at an international level can be found in the 1948 Universal Declaration of Human Rights, which specifically protects territorial and communications privacy. Article 12 states:

'No one should be subjected to arbitrary interference with his privacy, family, home or correspondence, nor to attacks on his honour or reputation. Everyone has the right to the protection of the law against such interferences or attacks.'

Numerous international human rights treaties specifically recognise privacy as a right. The International Covenant on Civil and Political Rights (ICCPR), Article 17, the United Nations (UN) Convention on Migrant Workers, Article 14, and the UN Convention on Protection of the Child, Article 16, adopt the same language.

On the regional level, various treaties make these rights legally enforceable. Article 8 of the European Convention for the Protection of Human Rights and Fundamental Freedoms 1950 (ECHR) states:

(1) Everyone has the right to respect for his private and family life, his home and his correspondence.

(2) There shall be no interference by a public authority with the exercise of this right except as in accordance with the law and is necessary in a democratic society in the interests of national security, public safety or the economic well-being of the country, for the prevention of disorder or crime, for the protection of health or morals, or for the protection of the rights and freedoms of others.

The Convention created the European Commission of Human Rights and the European Court of Human Rights to oversee enforcement. Both have been active in the enforcement of privacy rights and have consistently viewed Article 8's protections expansively and interpreted the restrictions narrowly. The Commission found in 1976:

For numerous Anglo-Saxon and French authors, the right to respect 'private life' is the right to privacy, the right to live, as far as one wishes, protected from publicity... In the opinion of the Commission, however, the right to respect for private life does not end there. It comprises also, to a certain degree, the right to establish and develop relationships with other human beings, especially in the emotional field for the development and fulfilment of one's own personality.

The Court has reviewed member states' laws and imposed sanctions on numerous countries for failing to regulate wiretapping by governments and private individuals. It has also reviewed cases of individuals' access to their personal information in government files to ensure that adequate procedures exist. It has expanded the protections of Article 8 beyond government actions to those of private persons where it appears that the government should have prohibited those actions.

Other regional treaties are also beginning to be used to protect privacy. Article 11 of the American Convention on Human Rights sets out the right to privacy in terms similar to the Universal Declaration. In 1965, the Organisation of American States proclaimed the American Declaration of the Rights and Duties of Man, which called for the protection of numerous human rights, including privacy. The Inter-American Court of Human Rights has begun to address privacy issues in its cases.

16 December 2007

↳ The above information is reprinted with kind permission from Privacy International. Visit www.privacyinternational.org for more information.

© *Privacy International*

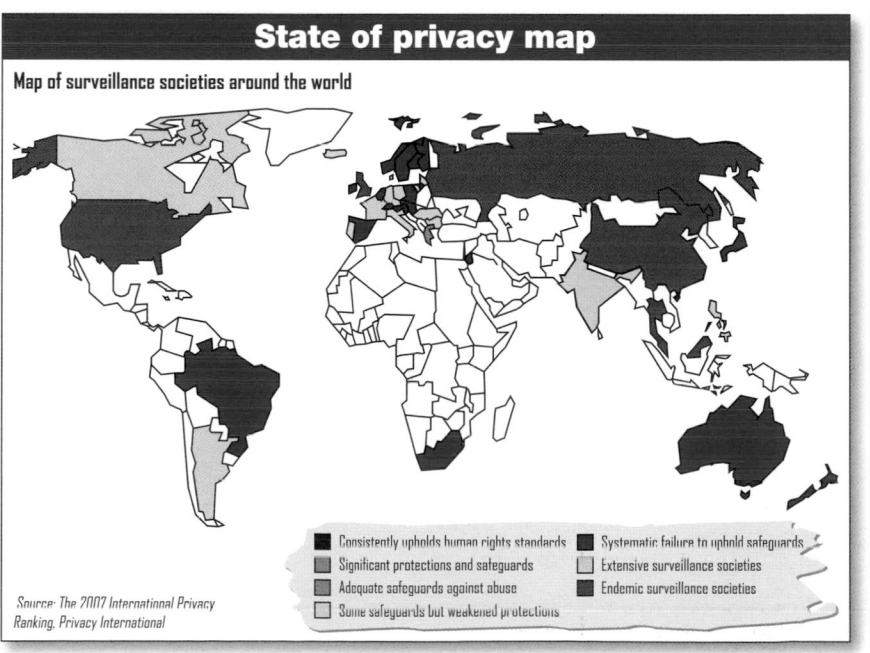

State of privacy map

Map of surveillance societies around the world

- ■ Consistently upholds human rights standards
- ■ Significant protections and safeguards
- ■ Adequate safeguards against abuse
- □ Some safeguards but weakened protections
- ■ Systematic failure to uphold safeguards
- □ Extensive surveillance societies
- ■ Endemic surveillance societies

Source: The 2007 International Privacy Ranking, Privacy International

A Surveillance Society?

Privacy and safeguards

By Anthony Hildebrand

The House of Commons Home Affairs Committee published its 'A Surveillance Society?' report on June 8. We present some of its key conclusions and recommendations in several instalments. Here's part one (further instalments are available via the Info4Secutiry website: www.info4secutiry.com)...

The report rejects 'crude characterisations of our society as a surveillance society in which all collections and means of collecting information about citizens are networked and centralised in the service of the state'.

Yet, it says, 'the potential for surveillance of citizens in public spaces and private communications has increased to the extent that ours could be described as a surveillance society unless trust in the Government's intentions in relation to data and data sharing is preserved. The Home Office in particular and Government in general must take every possible step to maintain and build on this trust: our Report provides a starting point.'

The report recommends that the Information Commissioner presents an annual report on surveillance to Parliament, and that the Government produces a response to the report, also to be presented to Parliament. It also recommends 'that Parliament have the opportunity to hold an annual debate on this issue'.

It notes that technology has advanced so that private and public sector service providers can target and facilitate access to service and products, but believes 'the elimination of technological barriers to the collection, storage and sharing of large volumes of information, however, has significant implications for individual privacy and potentially for society at large'.

'The Government should be open about its intentions in relation to collecting personal information, and should make sufficient time for public and Parliamentary debate on its proposals. In general the Government should move to curb the drive to collect more personal information and establish larger databases.'

> **'The Government should move to curb the drive to collect more personal information and establish larger databases'**

Increased risks

The report says that 'the risks associated with surveillance increase with the range and volume of information collected. The Government has a crucial role to play in maintaining the trust of the public: any evaluation of the use of surveillance must take into account the potential risk to this relationship with the public.'

It says the drive to make the most of technological capabilities should be tempered by an evaluation of the risks involved in collecting more information.

'Particular consideration should be given to situations in which individuals might suffer as a result of their lack of awareness or ability to take advantage of opportunities to exercise choice over how information about them is used, or to check that it is accurate,' the report says.

The report recommends that the Government 'track and make full use of new developments in encryption and other privacy-enhancing technologies and in particular those which limit the disclosure and collection of information which could identify individuals. We further recommend that the resources of the Information Commissioner's Office be expanded to accommodate sufficient technical expertise to be able to work with the Chief Information Officer to provide advice on the deployment of privacy-enhancing technologies in Government.'

Raising public awareness

The report says the Home Office should work with the Information Commissioner to raise public aware-

ness of 'how the Home Office collects, stores, shares and uses personal information. The Home Office should highlight the distinction between those areas in which individuals can exercise choice by giving or withholding their consent, and those areas in which seeking informed consent is not feasible and transparency is particularly important.'

It recommends that the Government 'adopt a principle of data minimisation in its policy and in the design of its systems. We further recommend that the Government acknowledge the distinction between identification and authentication as one which is valuable in its efforts to adhere to this principle.'

'The potential for surveillance of citizens in public spaces and private communications has increased to the extent that ours could be described as a surveillance society'

It also says information should only be held for as long as is necessary to fulfil the purpose for which it was collected – if needed for a secondary purpose it should be 'anonymised' and retained only for a specified period.

It welcomes reviews commissioned by the Government to improve data security, expects it to reassess 'the adequacy of the definitions and principles set out in the Data Protection Act. Such a reassessment should be carried out not only in light of recent data loss incidents but also against the challenges presented by increases in the collection, storage and sharing capability of information systems and intensification in criminal activity associated with the misuse of personal information. The Home Office must act as a matter of urgency to tackle these challenges.'

'Any increase in the collection and storage of information increases the

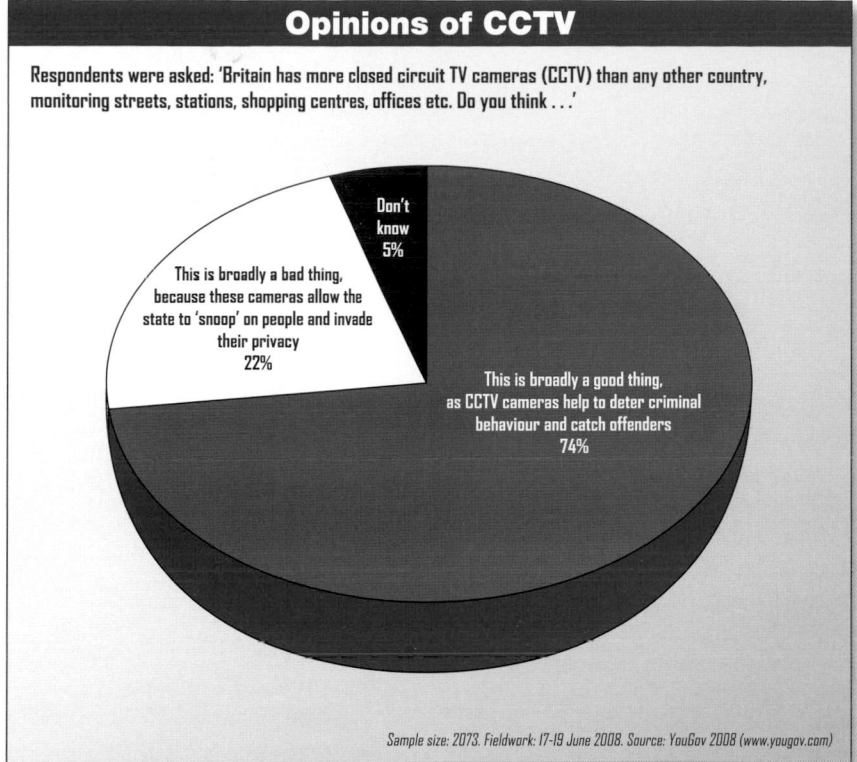

Opinions of CCTV

Respondents were asked: 'Britain has more closed circuit TV cameras (CCTV) than any other country, monitoring streets, stations, shopping centres, offices etc. Do you think ...'

Don't know 5%

This is broadly a bad thing, because these cameras allow the state to 'snoop' on people and invade their privacy 22%

This is broadly a good thing, as CCTV cameras help to deter criminal behaviour and catch offenders 74%

Sample size: 2073. Fieldwork: 17-19 June 2008. Source: YouGov 2008 (www.yougov.com)

risk that security will be breached and that information will be used for purposes other than those for which it was collected,' the report says.

'In keeping with a principle of data minimisation, more rigorous risk analysis of systems already in place must be carried out before new techniques for collecting information are deployed or new databases planned. The decision to create a major new database, share information on databases, or implement proposals for increased surveillance should be based on a proven need.'

Designing it in

The report places an emphasis on 'designing in' security and privacy in every system for collecting and storing personal information and data. It also says that 'for existing and proposed systems the Government should specify what it considers to be an acceptable level of failure and develop contingency plans to mitigate the damage caused by leaks or theft of data'.

'The weakest aspect of a system may be the establishment and enforcement of protocols for access and use rather than any technological safeguard,' the report says. 'Organisations which manage such systems must take full responsibility for limiting access to

databases and the information they contain and for enforcing procedures for sharing and transferring data.

'We support the Information Commissioner's call for an extension of his inspection and audit powers to facilitate the strengthening of these procedures across Government and the private sector. Tougher penalties for negligent information handling should be introduced in order to make clear where the burden of responsibility lies.

'A privacy officer or director of data security should be assigned by departments to take responsibility for risk analysis and to report to the Permanent Secretary on the privacy implications and safeguards of each project which involves the collection or sharing of personal information.

'The Home Office should publish a report on an audit of the data collections managed by the Department and its agencies, outlining as far as possible without compromising security the technological and procedural safeguards currently in place.'
11 June 2008

⇨ The above information is reprinted with kind permission from Info4Security. Visit www.info4security.com for more information.

© Info4Security

Overlooked

Surveillance and personal privacy in modern Britain

By Gareth Crossman

The past decade has brought many threats to personal privacy. However, over the last two years in particular, growing nervousness in Westminster, the media and wider public opinion suggests that the time may be ripe for broad and balanced debate about this important democratic value.

The contrast between the final years of the 1990s and the start of the current decade is marked. The right to respect for privacy became enforceable in UK courts as recently as October 2000 via the Human Rights Act 1998. However, the political context at the time gave privacy a difficult inception. The murder of Jamie Bulger in 1993, and the subsequent use of CCTV to help identify and convict his killers, struck a powerful chord with the public. Although there was little evidence that CCTV would actually deter crime, it became largely accepted with little debate over effectiveness or lack of regulation.

Within a year of the new privacy protections, the tragic events of 11 September 2001 served further to entrench a belief that concerns over privacy were automatically trumped by the demands of national security. 'Nothing to hide, nothing to fear' became a well-worn mantra.

So what has changed? No single dramatic event has increased interest in privacy. Rather a series of factors have combined to swing the pendulum back towards this concern. The flagship ID card programme and other huge public IT projects have been regularly challenged over cost and efficacy. The media debate has developed so that privacy and crime-fighting imperatives are no longer seen as a simple trade-off. Further, the Information Commissioner's Office (ICO) has regularly voiced concerns over the lack of effective privacy protection and regulation.

The UK is the world leader in CCTV use with approximately 4.2 million cameras in operation

Unfortunately, this late interest in privacy means that protection does not match the challenges of 2007. Data protection laws have become outdated and fail to keep pace with the reality of modern data processing;

CCTV remains largely unregulated; expansion of the National DNA Database (NDNAD) has continued apace; targeted state surveillance has also grown and remains under-regulated.

An overhaul of privacy protection is needed. This report makes a series of recommendations intended to improve the framework. This is not intended to champion privacy at the expense of crime detection, national security or other vital aims of the state. Rather it sets out to provide a proper regulatory regime, effective enforcement and improved accountability.

The report covers several forms of surveillance and their impact upon privacy. In particular the focus is on the Right to Respect for Privacy contained in Article 8 HRA and the framework of the Data Protection Act 1998 (DPA). The summary of findings and the most significant recommendations are as follows.

Targeted surveillance

This section considers the framework of state-sanctioned surveillance against specific targets created under the Regulation of Investigatory Powers Act 2000. Surveillance takes place on a massive scale with nearly 440,000 authorisations for communications traffic data taking place between June 2005 and March 2006. The report concludes that although the basic structure is sound it lacks accountability and transparency. In particular, there is a need for judicial authorisation for the most intrusive forms of surveillance and an improved complaints mechanism. Further, the bar on intercepted material in criminal trials needs to be lifted.

Mass surveillance

The sheer growth and impact of mass databases has been a significant development over the last decade. Increasingly the boundary between mass and targeted surveillance is blurring due to the increased use of

mass automated processes such as data mining and data matching. New data protection legislation is needed to allow better regulation of data and to improve the ability and resource of the ICO to provide effective enforcement. There should be greater accountability to parliament.

The right to respect for privacy became enforceable in UK courts as recently as October 2000

Visual surveillance

Daily exposure to mass CCTV surveillance is an all-pervading reality of 2007. The UK is the world leader in CCTV use with approximately 4.2 million cameras in operation. While CCTV has its uses, primarily in relation to crime detection, it remains relatively unevaluated in relation to crime prevention and cost effectiveness. The DPA fails to provide an effective enforcement tool. Compliance with more detailed guidance, such as that issued by the ICO, remains unenforceable and is largely dependent on proactive

and responsible attitudes from individual local authorities and police authorities. New legislation is needed to effectively regulate CCTV.

DNA

While there is a justification for the NDNAD, it is increasingly of concern. With an estimated 3.9 million samples, the NDNAD is five times larger than any other national database and contains samples taken from many who have never been convicted of any offence. This is largely due to successive acts of parliament rolling out the grounds for permanent retention to the current position where DNA can be taken and retained following arrest for any recordable offence. Expansion of the NDNAD by taking samples upon arrest rather than conviction has disproportionately affected black men with nearly 40% of black men represented, versus 13% of Asian men and 9% of white men. The effectiveness of mass roll-out of the NDNAD is questionable, with no statistical evidence that expansion has improved crime-solving rates. This is largely explained by the fact that DNA is of relevance only to a small number of criminal offences, mainly those involving sexual assault or other violence. There should be no further roll-out of the grounds for retention.

Samples should be deleted unless a person is convicted of a relevant offence or where there remains an ongoing investigation.

Privacy and the media

Developments in privacy law differ from other areas in this study. Rather than involving consideration of the legitimate limits of the relationship between the individual and the state developed through statute, it has tended to involve common law resolution between private parties. Privacy and the media has also usually more directly involved consideration of potentially conflicting rights, typically setting Article 8 (the Right to Respect for Privacy and Family Life) Rights against Article 10 (the Right to Free Expression). The result has been a sometimes confusing array of competing caselaw.

By Gareth Crossman, with Hilary Kitchin, Rekha Kuna Michael Skrein and Jago Russell.
October 2007

⇨ The above information is the executive summary of the report *Overlooked: Surveillance and personal privacy in modern Britain*, and is reprinted with kind permission from Liberty (www.liberty-human-rights.org.uk).
© Liberty

How Big Brother watches your every move

In our ever-growing surveillance society, the average Briton is being recorded 3,000 times a week. Richard Gray reports

With every telephone call, swipe of a card and click of a mouse, information is being recorded, compiled and stored about Britain's citizens.

An investigation by *The Sunday Telegraph* has now uncovered just how much personal data is being collected about individuals by the Government, law enforcement agencies and private companies each day.

In one week, the average person living in Britain has 3,254 pieces of

personal information stored about him or her, most of which is kept in databases for years and in some cases indefinitely.

The data include details about shopping habits, mobile phone use, emails, locations during the day, journeys and Internet searches.

In many cases this information is kept by companies such as banks and shops, but in certain circumstances they can be asked to hand it over to a range of legal authorities.

Britain's information watchdog, the Information Commissioner's Office, has called for tighter regulation of the amount of data held about citizens and urged the public to restrict the information they allow organisations to hold on them.

This newspaper's findings come days after the Government published plans to grant local authorities and other public bodies access to the email and Internet records of millions. Phone companies already retain data about their customers and give it to 650 public bodies on request.

The loss of data by Government departments, including an incident where HM Revenue and Customs mislaid computer disks containing the personal details of 25 million people, has heightened concerns about the amount of information being stored.

David Smith, deputy information commissioner, said: 'As more and more information is collected and kept on all of us, we are very concerned that appropriate safeguards go along with that.

'People should know what is happening with their information and have a choice.

'Our concern is that what is kept with the justification of preventing and detecting terrorism, can then be used for minor purposes such as pursuing people for parking fines.'

Earlier this year the Commons home affairs select committee recommended new controls and regulations on the accumulation of information by the state.

Mobile phone users are potentially subject to a range of privacy intrusions

Mobile phones
Every day the average person makes three mobile phone calls and sends at least two text messages.

Each time the network provider logs information about who was called as well as the caller's location and direction of travel, worked out by triangulation from phone masts.

Customers can also have their locations tracked even when they are not using their phones, as the devices send out unique identifying signals at regular intervals.

All of this information can be accessed by police and other public authorities investigating crimes.

The Internet
Internet service providers (ISPs) compile information about their customers when they go online, including name, address, the unique identification number for the connection, known as an IP address, any browser used and location.

They also keep details of emails, such as whom they were sent to, together with the date and time they were sent. An average of 50 websites are visited and 32 emails sent per person in Britain every day.

In one week, the average person living in Britain has 3,254 pieces of personal information stored about him or her, most of which is kept in databases for years

---

Privacy campaigners have expressed concern that the country's three biggest ISPs – BT, Virgin Media and TalkTalk – now provide this data to a digital advertising company called Phorm so that it can analyse web surfing habits.

ISPs are already voluntarily providing information they hold about their customers if requested by law enforcement agencies and public authorities. A consultation published last week by the Government would make it a legal requirement for ISPs to provide a customer's personal in-formation when requested. A total of 520,000 requests were made by public officials for telephone and Internet details last year, an increase from around 350,000 the previous year.

Internet search engines also compile data about their users, including the IP address and what was searched for. Google receives around 68 searches from the average person each day and stores this data for 18 months.

Dr Ian Brown, a research fellow on privacy at Oxford University, said: 'Companies such as Google and Internet service providers are

building up huge databases of data about Internet users.

'These companies may be compelled, through a legal action, to hand over this information to third parties or the Government, or the companies may lose the data and it can then be misused.'

Loyalty cards
Store 'loyalty' cards also retain large amounts of information about individuals who have signed up to use them. They link a person's personal details to the outlets used, the transaction times and how much is spent.

In the case of Nectar cards, which are used by more than 10 million people in Britain once a week, information from dozens of shops is compiled, giving a detailed picture of a cardholder's shopping habits.

A spokesman for Loyalty Management UK, which runs the Nectar programme, insisted that information about the items bought was not compiled, but some partners in the scheme, such as Sainsbury's, use their till records to compile that information.

She admitted that the personal information that is compiled under the Nectar scheme is kept indefinitely until individuals close their account and ask for their information to be destroyed. In criminal inquiries, police can request the details held by Nectar.

Banks
Banks can also be required to hand over personal account information to the authorities if requested as part of an investigation.

They also provide personal data to credit reference agencies, debt collectors and fraud prevention organisations.

Debit and credit card transactions can give information about where and on what people are spending their money.

CCTV
The biggest source of surveillance in Britain is through the network of CCTV (closed-circuit television) cameras. On average, an individual will appear on 300 CCTV cameras during a day and those tapes are kept

by many organisations for indefinite lengths of time.

On the London Underground network, Transport for London (TfL) keeps footage for a minimum of 14 days. TfL operates more than 8,500 CCTV cameras in its underground stations, 1,550 cameras on tube trains and up to 60,000 cameras on buses.

Network Rail refused to say how many CCTV cameras it operates or for how long the footage is kept.

Britain now has more CCTV cameras in public spaces than any other country in the world. A study in 2002 estimated that there were around 4.2 million cameras, but that number is likely to now be far higher.

Number plate recognition

The latest development in CCTV is the increased use of automatic number plate recognition systems, which read number plates and search databases for signs that a vehicle has been used in crime.

A national automatic number plate recognition system is maintained by the Association of Chief Police Officers along motorways and main roads. Every number plate picked up by the system is stored in a database with date, time and location for two years.

Public transport

Travel passes such as the Oyster Card used in London and the Key card, in Oxford, can also reveal remarkable amounts of information about an individual. When they are registered to a person's name, they record journey history, dates, times and fares.

A spokesman for TfL, which runs the Oyster Card system, insisted that access to this information was restricted to its customer services agents.

Police, however, can also obtain this information and have used Oyster Card journey records as evidence in criminal cases.

The workplace

Employers are increasingly using radio-tagged security passes for employees, providing them with information about when staff enter and leave the office.

17 August 2008

© *Telegraph Group Limited, London 2008*

Surveillance in the EU

EU is set to become the most surveilled place in the world

EU laws on driving licences have been harmonised so that licences have to be renewed initially every 10 years with the option for every five years – in the UK a driving licence is held from passing the test until the age of 70 (when it can be renewed with a doctor's letter). Renewing the licence every 10 years will mean the 'chip' and the data on it can be updated and adapted.

In the UK a National Health database will hold the records of all 60 million people with over 350,000 'clinicians' having access – as will police and security agencies. The EU is planning a new EU Health Card and argue the benefits of being able to travel anywhere with your medical details available.

The EU is keen too on 'e-government' cards and much research is being conducted. 'E-government' gives people access to state services where they have to prove who they are, for example, to get medical or hospital treatment, local government services like libraries, getting social and unemployment benefits and so on.

The day may not be far off when all these state-run systems will be put on one card: passport, ID card, driving licence, health record and e-government.

The Schengen Information System (SIS) is to be upgraded to hold more categories of data (including fingerprints and DNA), access to all the data is to be extended to all agencies (police, immigration and customs).[1] SIS II is to share a 'common technical platform' with VIS (Visa Information System) for the policing of visitors – thus SIS II/VIS will become a dedicated surveillance tool.[2]

Discussions to create an EU-PNR (passenger name record) system are under way. In June 2008 the Council threw the Commission proposal out and in the autumn it will draw up its own draft. A number of governments do not like limiting the use of data to terrorism and organised crime and want to extend the proposal's scope from just in and out of the EU to travel between EU states and even within each state. The same view also supports extending the scope from air travel to land and sea travel too.

An EU entry-exit system is planned for third country nationals entering with visas, and those without visas too, as is an EU version of an Electronic System for Travel Authorisation (ESTA). The former proposal includes the automated checking of EU citizens – that is, passports and biometrics (fingerprints) to be checked by 'machines' not people. The EU-PNR exit-entry system and ESTA will put the EU on the same footing as the USA.

The Prum Treaty, agreed by 17 EU member states, has led to the incorporation of the policing aspects into EU law (the automated exchange of DNA, fingerprint and vehicle data) thus applying across all 27 member states. The immigration aspects – including the use of air marshals – are being adopted by the signatory states.

Notes

1 *Lex Vigilatoria – Towards a control system without a state?* by Thomas Mathiesen: http://www.ecln.org/essays/essay-7.pdf
2 *SIS II fait accompli? Construction of EU's Big Brother database underway:* http://www.statewatch.org/analyses/no-45-sisII-analysis-may05.pdf
October 2008

⇨ The above information is an extract from the report *The Shape of Things to Come – the EU Future Group* (published by Spokesman Books) and is reprinted with kind permission from Statewatch. Visit www.statewatch.org for more information.

© *Statewatch*

Checks on surveillance

Information from the Home Office

The use of surveillance is carefully regulated, as the misuse of surveillance techniques can have serious consequences for our civil rights.

Laws regulating the use of surveillance

In the UK, our civil rights concerning surveillance are protected by:

⇨ Regulation of Investigatory Powers Act 2000 (RIPA).

⇨ Article 8 of the European Convention on Human Rights, which states that everyone has the right to respect for his or her private and family life, home and correspondence.

⇨ Data Protection Act 1998.

⇨ Covert Surveillance Code of Practice.

⇨ Interception of Communications Code of Practice.

More information on the Regulation of Investigatory Powers Act 2000 can be found on the Home Office Security website (http://security.homeoffice.gov.uk/ripa).

These pieces of legislation safeguard our rights by:

Necessitating approval at the highest level

Interception warrants require the personal approval of the Secretary of State who must believe the warrant is necessary in the interests of national security, preventing or detecting serious crime, or safeguarding the UK's economic well-being.

Limiting use of information obtained through surveillance

With a few exceptions the law does not allow any information gained from interception to be used as evidence in court. The only exceptions are for offences relating to interception – for example Official Secrets Act offences.

Requiring an independent watchdog

The interception warrant system is overseen by an independent Interception of Communications Commissioner who ensures that authorised agencies have proper processes in place, and have considered the human rights of individuals before interception takes place.

The Investigatory Powers Tribunal hears complaints from members of the public about inappropriate interception activities by any of the intelligence services or by public authorities.

Insisting that the surveillance method must fit the crime

Authorising officers must consider whether the level of surveillance is proportionate to the suspected crime – this means your home won't be bugged if you're seen dropping litter but it may be if you're a suspected terrorist.

Protecting others

Authorising officers must consider the risk of 'collateral intrusion', meaning the likelihood of obtaining private information about a person other than the surveillance target, before authorising surveillance or the acquistion of communications data.

Concerned about surveillance?

If you're worried that you've been put under surveillance by certain public authorities without good reason, you should contact the Investigatory Powers Tribunal.

⇨ The above information is reprinted with kind permission from the Home Office. Visit www.homeoffice.gov.uk for more information.

© Crown copyright

Freedom of information and data protection

What's the difference?

Both the Data Protection Act 1998 and the Freedom of Information Act 2000 give people rights to see or receive information.

So what's the difference?

The Data Protection Act allows you to see the personal information that is held about you by organisations of all types – such as the NHS in the public sector or your bank in the private sector. Examples of personal information include your name, address and telephone number, your bank account number, your medical records and the things you buy when you are shopping.

The Freedom of Information Act gives you rights to see official information held by public authorities such as local councils, hospitals and the police. For example, you could ask your local council for information about hygiene inspections in local restaurants or ask a university for exam pass rates.

Personal information

The Data Protection Act places responsibilities on organisations that hold your personal information to:

⇨ use it fairly;

⇨ keep it secure;

⇨ make sure it's accurate; and

⇨ keep it up to date.

You have the right under the Data Protection Act to have your information corrected if it is wrong. You also have the right to claim compensation through the courts if an organisation breaches the Act and this causes you damage, such as financial loss. If it has, you can also claim for distress.

The Data Protection Act and the Privacy and Electronic Communications Regulations also give you the right to stop your personal information being used for any sort of direct marketing, such as unwanted junk mail, sales calls, or email and text messages. This means that in most cases organisations should ask you before they use your information to send you marketing messages.

Official information

The Freedom of Information Act 2000 applies to public authorities in England, Wales and Northern Ireland and to those which are UK-wide.

Similar but separate legislation applies to Scottish public authorities. For more information about the Freedom of Information (Scotland) Act 2002 visit the Office of the Scottish Information Commissioner at www.itspublicknowledge.info.

The Freedom of Information Act aims to promote openness in the public sector, which includes government departments, councils, hospitals, schools and the police. The Act helps the public to get a better understanding of how public authorities carry out their duties, why they make their decisions, and how they spend public money.

In addition to the Freedom of Information Act, the Environmental Information Regulations give you the right to request information about the environment which is held by public authorities.

⇨ The above information is reprinted with kind permission from the Information Commissioner's Office. Visit www.ico.gov.uk for more.

© Information Commissioner's Office

The national DNA database

Information from the Home Office

The national DNA database is a key police intelligence tool that helps to:

⇨ quickly identify offenders;

⇨ make earlier arrests;

⇨ secure more convictions;

⇨ provide critical investigative leads for police investigations.

DNA samples obtained for analysis from the collection of DNA at crime scenes and from samples taken from individuals in police custody can be held in the national DNA database.

The UK's database is the largest of any country: 5.2% of the UK population is on the database compared with 0.5% in the USA. The database has expanded significantly over the last five years. By the end of 2005 over 3.4 million DNA profiles were held on the database – the profiles of the majority of the known active offender population.

This expansion and investment is being closely followed by Europe and America who are keen to emulate the crime-solving successes of the database.

Maintaining and developing the database is one of the government's top priorities, with government and police investment of over £300million over the last five years. However, there are no plans to introduce a universal compulsory or voluntary DNA database.

Oversight of the database

A Home Office unit is responsible for regulating the database. This work is overseen by a board composed of the Home Office, the Association of Chief Police Officers and the Association of Police Authorities. The Human Genetics Commission are also represented on the board, and there are plans to establish an ethics group to contribute and offer advice.

The government retained control of the database from the Forensic Science Service in December 2005, when the Forensic Science Service became a GovCo.

Why are people who have not been convicted on the database?

Before 2001, the police could take DNA samples during investigations but had to destroy the samples and the records derived from them on the database if the people concerned were acquitted or charges were not proceeded with.

The law was changed in 2001 to remove this requirement, and changed again in 2004 so that DNA samples could be taken from anyone arrested for a recordable offence and detained in a police station.

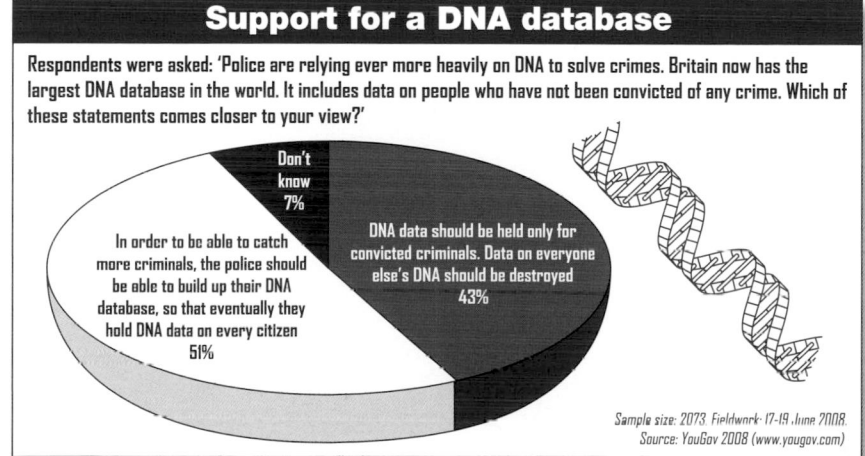

Support for a DNA database

Respondents were asked: 'Police are relying ever more heavily on DNA to solve crimes. Britain now has the largest DNA database in the world. It includes data on people who have not been convicted of any crime. Which of these statements comes closer to your view?'

Don't know 7%

In order to be able to catch more criminals, the police should be able to build up their DNA database, so that eventually they hold DNA data on every citizen 51%

DNA data should be held only for convicted criminals. Data on everyone else's DNA should be destroyed 43%

Sample size: 2073. Fieldwork: 17-19 June 2008.
Source: YouGov 2008 (www.yougov.com)

Does this pose any privacy problems?

Any intrusion on personal privacy is proportionate to the benefits that are gained.

By the end of 2005, about 200,000 samples had been retained that would have been destroyed before the 2001 change in legislation. 8,000 of these samples matched with DNA taken from crime scenes, involving nearly 14,000 offences, including murders and rapes.

In 2005-06 45,000 crimes were matched against records on the DNA database; including 422 homicides (murders and manslaughters) and 645 rapes.

Are under-18s disproportionately represented?

No. Under-18s make up 23% of all arrests, and so a comparative proportion of profiles is to be expected. There are no legal powers to take a DNA sample from anyone under ten without the consent of a parent or legal guardian.

⇨ The above information is reprinted with kind permission from the Home Office. Visit www.homeoffice. gov.uk for more information.

© Crown copyright

Britons win DNA landmark decision

Information from MSN News

All DNA evidence taken during criminal proceedings in England and Wales is currently retained.

Nearly a million innocent people could have their records removed from the national DNA database after a court ruled holding them breached their human rights.

The European Court of Human Rights severely criticised police powers to take and hold samples from suspects even if they are released or cleared.

Home Secretary Jacqui Smith said she was disappointed with the ruling and would consider it carefully before responding.

The result is a victory for two Britons who have been fighting to change the law after police insisted on retaining their DNA records.

Michael Marper, 45, was arrested in March 2001 and charged with harassing his partner, but the case was dropped three months later after the two were reconciled. He had no previous convictions. In a separate case, a 19-year-old named in court only as 'S' was arrested and charged with attempted robbery in January 2001 when he was 12, but he was cleared five months later.

The men, both from Sheffield, asked that their fingerprints, DNA samples and profiles be destroyed. South Yorkshire Police refused, saying the details would be retained 'to aid criminal investigation'.

The men's claims were later thrown out by the House of Lords, which ruled that keeping the information was not illegal under the Criminal Justice and Police Act, and did not breach human rights.

But earlier this year, when the cases came before the Human Rights Court, lawyers for the two men argued that keeping the DNA of innocent citizens left them under a cloud of suspicion.

It violated their 'right to respect for private life' and 'prohibition of discrimination' safeguarded by the Human Rights Convention, to which the UK is a signatory.

The verdict from the European Court of Human Rights could force the Government to remove the DNA details of hundreds of thousands of Britons from the current total of about 4.5 million held on the England, Wales and Northern Ireland database.

4 December 2008

⇨ The above information is reprinted with kind permission from MSN. Visit www.msn.com for more information.

© MSN

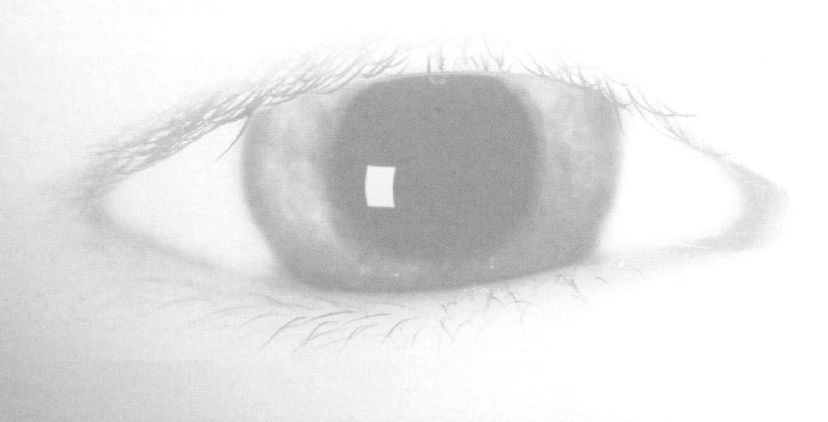

Biometric travel documents

Information from the UK Border Agency

From 17 March 2008 the Home Office will be issuing biometric travel documents. The process of applying for a Home Office travel document will not change. All applications must be made by post by completing a travel document application form (TD112 Revision 12) and enclosing the correct fee and supporting documents.

The biometric travel document contains the holder's details on a tamper-proof bio-chip

---

What is a biometric travel document?

The biometric travel document has a new design and security features including a biometric chip. The chip contains the holder's details as shown on page 31 of the document. Only personal information shown on this page (name, nationality, sex, place and date of birth and signature) is included on the chip. The applicant's scanned photograph is the biometric element of the document. No other information is included on the chip.

How secure is the biometric travel document – who will have access to my biometric details?

The biometric travel document contains the holder's details on a tamper-proof biometric chip. All United Kingdom immigration ports and European Union (EU) member states have the capability to read the data on the bio-chip.

How long are the biometric travel documents valid for?

There will be no change to validity of Home Office travel documents as a result of the introduction of biometrics.

Will my current document still be valid?

You can still use your current travel document until it expires. If you apply for and are issued with a new document after 17 March 2008 you will receive a biometric travel document.

How much will it cost?

Fees for Home Office travel documents will not change with the introduction of the new biometric documents. They will however be subject to yearly review as with the current travel document.

Changes to the certificate of identity

From 17 March 2008 the certificate of identity will change its name to the certificate of travel. The colour of the document will change from brown to black. The validity and criteria for issuing the document will not change. If you currently hold a brown certificate of identity document, you can still use it until it expires.
10 March 2008

⇨ The above information is reprinted with kind permission from the UK Border Agency. Visit http://ukba.homeoffice.gov.uk for more.
© *Crown copyright*

A step too far?

A communications database would be 'a step too far'

Any government-run database holding the telephone and Internet communications of the entire population would raise serious data protection concerns, the Information Commissioner, Richard Thomas, is warning today. Commenting on speculation that the government is considering the development of such a database Richard Thomas will say that it would be 'a step too far for the British way of life'.

Speaking at the launch of his annual report, Richard Thomas will say: 'I am absolutely clear that the targeted, and duly authorised, interception of the communications of suspects can be invaluable in the fight against terrorism and other serious crime. But there needs to be the fullest public debate about the justification for, and implications of, a specially-created database – potentially accessible to a wide range of law enforcement authorities – holding details of everyone's telephone and Internet communications. Do we really want the police, security services and other organs of the state to have access to more and more aspects of our private lives?

'Speculation that the Home Office is considering collecting this information from phone companies and Internet service providers has been reinforced by the government's Draft Legislative Programme which, referring to a proposed Communications Data Bill, talks

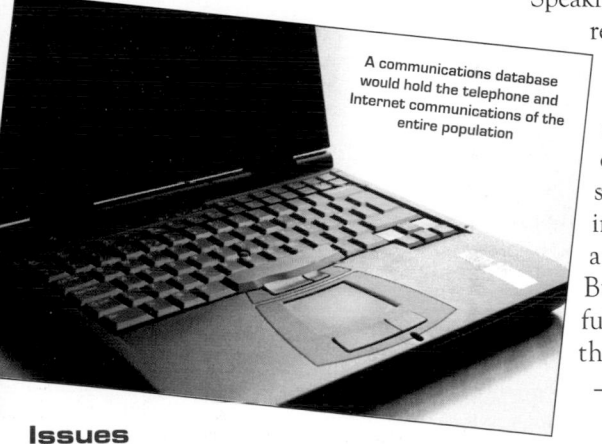

A communications database would hold the telephone and Internet communications of the entire population

about "modifying procedures for acquiring communications data".'

Richard Thomas believes that there has not been sufficient parliamentary or public debate on proposals to collect more and more personal information without proper justification, citing the expansion of the DNA database and the centralised collection and retention of data from Automatic Number Plate Recognition (ANPR) cameras as two recent examples.

Richard Thomas says: 'We welcomed last month's report from the all-party Home Affairs Committee warning of the dangers of excessive surveillance. I entirely agree that before major new databases are launched careful consideration must be given to the impact on individuals' liberties and on society as a whole. Sadly, there have been too many developments where there has not been sufficient openness, transparency or public debate.'

The Information Commissioner's Office (ICO) is today serving enforcement notices against HMRC and MoD following recent high profile data breaches. The notices require both departments to provide progress reports documenting in detail how the recommendations have been, or are being, implemented to improve Data Protection compliance. Failure to comply with an Enforcement Notice is a criminal offence.

The Information Commissioner's annual report highlights that the ICO received 24,851 enquiries and complaints concerning personal information in 2007/8. The ICO has prosecuted 11 individuals and organisations in the last 12 months.

The ICO received 2,646 freedom of information complaints over the last year and closed 2,658. Three hundred and ninety-five formal Decision Notices were issued and of these, 30% ruled in favour of the complainant while 25% upheld public authorities' original decisions. In 45% of cases the ICO upheld some elements of the complaint in favour of the complainant and agreed with the public authority on others.
15 July 2008

⇨ The above information is reprinted with kind permission from the Information Commissioner's Office. Visit www.ico.gov.uk for more.
© *Information Commissioner's Office*

Benefits of the National Identity Scheme

Information from the Identity and Passport Service

Benefits at a glance

The potential benefits of the National Identity Scheme are wide-ranging. The following list shows you some of the key benefits at a glance.

The National Identity Scheme will:
⇨ help protect cardholders against identity theft and fraud;
⇨ provide a reliable way of checking the identity of people in positions of trust;
⇨ make travelling in Europe easier;
⇨ provide a secure way of applying for financial products and making financial transactions, including those made over the Internet;
⇨ offer a secure and convenient way of proving your age;
⇨ help to confirm your eligibility for public services and benefits – and reduce fraud relating to these services and benefits;
⇨ help in the prevention of organised crime and terrorism;
⇨ help combat illegal working and reduce illegal immigration to the UK;
⇨ allow the police more quickly to identify suspects and people they arrest.

Identity theft and fraud

Identity fraud is on the increase. As well as causing great distress to the victims, it costs the UK economy millions of pounds each year.

Criminals can copy personal information (from a bank statement, for example) or steal or forge the documents – such as utility bills – we currently use to prove identity.

The National Identity Scheme is designed to be far more secure than anything we use at present. Security is

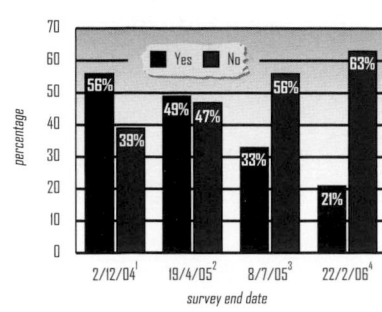
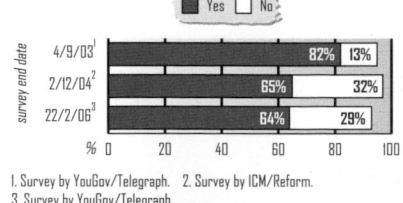

Changing opinion on usefulness of ID cards

Will ID cards help prevent terrorist attacks?
ICM: Agreement with statements: 'ID cards will help Britain to fight the war against terrorism', or 'ID cards did not help prevent the Madrid bombings so what difference would they make here?'
Populus: Do you think that the introduction of ID cards would help to prevent a terrorist attack?
YouGov: Do you think identity cards would, or would not, help in the future to prevent the commission of terrorist acts like those that were committed in London in July 2005?

1. Survey by ICM/Reform. 2. Survey by Populus/Times.
3. Survey by YouGov/Telegraph. 4. Follow-up survey by YouGov/Telegraph.

Will ID cards help tackle benefit fraud?
ICM: Agreement with statements: 'ID cards will help to prevent benefit fraud', or 'ID cards will inevitably be forged which will undermine their effectiveness against fraud'.
YouGov: A number of purposes have been suggested for identity cards. Do you think identity cards would or would not help to achieve the following objectives? Cut down on benefit fraud, by making it more difficult for people to claim state benefits they are not entitled to . . .

1. Survey by YouGov/Telegraph. 2. Survey by ICM/Reform.
3. Survey by YouGov/Telegraph.

Source: 'ID Cards', collated by UK Polling Report.

built in to the system in the following ways:

- ⇨ Biometric data is held both on the card and in the National Identity Register (NIR). A criminal may steal your card, but your unique biometric data cannot be taken from you. Anyone trying to make a major financial transaction, for example, would have their biometric data checked against that held in the NIR. If they were not the registered cardholder this check would fail.
- ⇨ Each ID card has a PIN known only to the cardholder.
- ⇨ Each card also has a biometric image of the cardholder's face. This looks like a photograph and can be used for a quick visual check that the customer presenting the card is the genuine cardholder.

We expect the increased security offered by the National Identity Scheme to:

- ⇨ make it far more difficult to commit identity theft and fraud;
- ⇨ act as a deterrent for the future;
- ⇨ make it much easier to catch and prosecute those who attempt identity theft and fraud.

Benefits for British citizens

Once it is up and running the National Identity Scheme could:

- ⇨ protect your identity from theft;
- ⇨ protect vulnerable people from those who have lied to gain positions of trust;
- ⇨ offer a convenient way to prove your age;
- ⇨ speed up many everyday transactions;
- ⇨ make it easier for you to travel in Europe;
- ⇨ make it simpler to prove your ID;
- ⇨ make the Internet easier to use;
- ⇨ make it easier to replace lost and stolen documents;
- ⇨ protect your privacy.

Protect your identity from theft

Identity theft or fraud involves someone using your identity to, for example, open bogus accounts, apply for loans, buy goods over the phone or Internet, or take over one of your bank accounts. By registering and using your card to prove who you are you will be able to protect yourself and help reduce identity theft. The National Identity Scheme is designed to be more secure than current ways of proving identity. It will make it extremely difficult for someone else to impersonate you, even if they have your ID card, because only you can be matched to your biometrics.

Will ID cards help to protect our identities, or obscure them?

Protect vulnerable people from those who have lied to gain positions of trust

You need to know that people in positions of trust (such as nannies, carers for the elderly, childminders, and so on) are who they say they are. Biometric data in the ID card means that a potential employer could quickly and reliably confirm an applicant's identity. The Criminal Records Bureau could also use the applicant's Identity Registration Number (IRN) in order to check that they have no criminal record, for example. Use of the IRN will speed up such searches significantly.

Offer a convenient and trusted way to prove your age

Whether you are a young person wanting to buy a drink in a pub or an older person who wishes to claim a travel discount, the easy-to-carry ID card will offer a safe and secure way to prove your age.

Speed up many everyday transactions

Once you are registered with the National Identity Scheme you will have a quick and secure way of proving your identity whenever you need to, for example via a match of your ID card and biometrics or PIN.

Make it easier for you to travel in Europe

With a UK ID card that shows your nationality you will be able to enter European countries without the need to carry your passport. The card will also reduce checking time at ports and borders.

Make it simpler to prove your identity

There will be no need to keep many different identity documents – just one convenient card that can be used only by you, since only you have the biometrics associated with your ID card. You won't need to carry the card with you at all times, and if you need to prove your identity without the card you will be able to do so by providing a few details about yourself along with a biometric, such as a fingerprint or PIN.

Make the Internet easier and safer to use

There will be less need to remember an array of user names and passwords – just use your ID card and PIN online. Your card will help you securely log on to services and also provide a digital 'signature'. With this you can authorise important transactions and application forms, giving both you and the service provider more confidence in the exchange.

Make it easier to replace lost and stolen documents

If you lose your ID card or passport, or if they are stolen, all you will need to do is to go to a local office where your identity can be checked against your biometrics. Your original documents will be cancelled so no one else can try to use them and replacements will be sent out to you.

Protect your privacy

The National Identity Scheme has been designed with your privacy in mind. Only the most basic information is contained on the card itself – more detailed identity information is held securely in the National Identity Register (NIR), and only accredited user organisations will be able to use the NIR to check your identity.

Some facts and figures

- ⇨ Identity fraud has cost the UK over £1.7 billion.

- CIFAS, the UK's Fraud Prevention Service, recorded 67,406 victims of identity fraud in 2006, up from 56,200 in 2005. Since 2000 almost 282,300 victims of identity fraud have been registered by CIFAS.
- Over 10,000 fraudulent passport applications each year.
- 430,000 illegal migrants could be living in the UK.
- Between £20 million and £50 million of identity-related benefit fraud is committed each year.

Terrorism and organised crime

Terrorists and criminals are known to use false and multiple identities to disguise their activities, avoid detection and 'launder' money.

The 'biographical footprint' check will make it extremely difficult to register with the National Identity Scheme under a false identity, and the scheme will not allow people to register more than once as their biometric data would be detected. While the National Identity Scheme cannot prevent terrorism, it can make it far more difficult for terrorists to conceal their identity.

The scheme will help the security services in their investigations into organised crime and terrorist activities and help protect the UK against threats to national security.

The National Identity Scheme can also be used by the police and security services for identification. For example, any fingerprints found at the scene of a crime (including unsolved crimes) that do not match existing police records could be identified by searching for a match in the biometric data held on the National Identity Register (NIR). This will greatly speed up investigations and may even lead to the identification of people involved in previously unsolved crimes.

Immigration and illegal working

There are an estimated 430,000 illegal migrants living in the UK, and employers currently have no reliable way of establishing whether or not a job applicant has a right to work here.

The National Identity Scheme will help employers find out about the immigration status of job applicants and about any visa restrictions which mean they cannot legally work in the UK. This will speed up the checking process and could be an advantage to those immigrants who are entitled to work. It could also help to identify people who try to work here illegally and could deter potential illegal immigrants from coming to the UK.

Delivery of public services and benefits

The National Identity Scheme will provide an easy and reliable way for people to prove their identity and thereby their entitlement to services and benefits. The systems that deliver services and benefits are currently open to abuse and the Department for Work and Pensions estimates that between £20 million and £50 million of identity-related benefit fraud is committed each year in the UK.

Fraud on this scale takes resources away from those most in need and is unfair to the millions of honest citizens who fund these services and benefits through tax and National Insurance payments.

The ID card will eventually replace the range of documents currently used for this purpose, making life simpler both for claimants and those responsible for checking their claims.

- The above information is reprinted with kind permission from the Identity and Passport Service. Visit www.ips.gov.uk for more information.
© Crown copyright

Public opinion on ID cards

NO2ID poll: public is 2 to 1 against the idea behind ID cards

Public opinion is split 50:50 on ID cards if asked a fair question; but ask people about the database that is the *raison d'être* for the National Identity Scheme, and opinion is two-to-one against. These are the findings of an ICM poll conducted for NO2ID last week.

NO2ID has been periodically asking the identical unbiased question about 'ID cards' since June 2005 – an approach described by UK Polling Report as 'admirable'. During that time support for the idea has steadily declined to 48%.

But as an experiment this time round they asked a second question, also designed to be fair, which did not mention ID cards but did describe the National Identity Register on which the scheme is to be built. The result? 63% of the public is opposed to the substance of the National Identity Scheme.

NO2ID recommends people look very closely at how the Home Office gets its nominally positive ratings for the scheme in its 'tracking studies'.

Phil Booth, NO2ID National Coordinator, said:

'Unlike the IPS we can't afford to waste money on spin dressed up as a poll. We care what people really think. We are trying to persuade them, not con them.

'What's fascinating here is that we asked the public two different-seeming questions that are about the same thing. One aspect, the card itself, bothers substantial numbers of people but not a big majority. But the more important part of the scheme – government collecting and collating information about us for its convenience – is just massively unpopular.

'Campaigning experience suggests that the more people know about the ID scheme, the more they dislike it. Now here is some solid evidence that it is true.'
30 June 2008

- The above information is reprinted with kind permission from the NO2ID campaign. Visit www.no2id.net for more information.
© The NO2ID campaign

ID card myths

Information from the Identity and Passport Service

You'll have to carry a card

You will not have to carry an ID card, although you may find it simple and convenient to do so. In fact the Act specifically prohibits making the carrying of an ID card compulsory.

The police can demand to see your card

The police have no new powers associated with the scheme and they will not be able to stop you and demand to see your card.

The money could be better spent on other public services

Approximately 80% of the costs incurred will be spent in any event on necessary security enhancements to passports. There is no 'pot of money' which could be spent on other things like 'bobbies on the beat' or prisons. Other than some of the initial set-up costs, the scheme will be funded, as with passports, mainly through fees charged to those applying.

The database will know everything about you

Only basic personal information will be held to prove your identity – such as name, nationality, age, address and gender. This is no different to what is already held by the public sector, e.g. for issuing National Insurance numbers and driving licences. Unrelated information such as religious beliefs, tax and medical records cannot be held. In fact there are strict limits in the legislation which expressly prevent this.

ID cards can stop global terrorism and crime

No one has ever claimed ID cards are a panacea for global terrorism or crime. But we do know they will make a contribution to tackling crimes such as illegal working, money laundering and benefit fraud, which are enabled by the possession of multiple identities. Terrorists are known to use multiple identities to avoid detection and hide their activities. ID cards will make it much harder for criminals to build up multiple fraudulent identities by securely linking one person's identity with one set of unique biometrics.

An ID card will cost £300

This figure is complete nonsense. We intend that the fee for an identity card in 2009 and 2010 will be £30 or less.

If the Government already has a lot of info on me, why do we need an ID card?

You are right that whether it is medical records, or information about your driving licence – the Government does hold information about individuals on specific issues. As do many private companies from Sky to Tesco. But what the Government does not have, and nor do you, is a fail-proof system that can prove you really are who you say you are. The long-established ways of linking us to our identity – a signature or a photograph – are no longer enough. ID cards will link your basic personal information to something uniquely yours – like the pattern of your iris, your face shape or your fingerprint. It will protect your identity from people fraudulently claiming to be you and make it easier for you to prove your identity when you need to – like opening a bank account, moving house, applying for benefits or starting a job.

⇨ The above information is reprinted with kind permission from the Identity and Passport Service. Visit www.ips. gov.uk for more information.

© Crown copyright

The problems with ID cards

Information from the NO2ID campaign

Not just a card. The card is the least of it…

The proposed identity management system has multiple layers

The NIR (National Identity Register) – individual checking and numbering of the population – marking many personal details as 'registrable facts' to be disclosed and constantly updated – collection and checking of biometrics (e.g. fingerprints) – the card itself – a widespread scanner network and secure (one hopes) infrastructure connecting it to the central database – provision for use

across the private and public sectors – data-sharing between organisations on an unprecedented scale.

Massive accumulation of personal data

50 categories of registrable fact are set out in the Bill, though they could be added to. Effectively an index to all other official and quasi-official records, through cross-references and an audit trail of all checks on the Register, the NIR would be the key to a total life history of every individual, to be retained even after death.

Lifelong surveillance and the meta-database

Every registered individual will be under an obligation to notify any change in registrable facts. It is a clear aim of the system to require identity verification for many more civil transactions, the occasions to be stored in the audit trail. Information verified and indexed by numbers from the NIR would be easily cross-referenced in any database or set of databases. The 'meta-database' of all the thousands of databases cross-referenced is much more powerful and much less secure than the NIR itself.

Overseas ID cards are not comparable

Many western countries that have ID cards do not have a shared register. Mostly ID cards have been limited in use, with strong legal privacy protections. In Germany centralisation is forbidden for historical reasons, and when cards are replaced, the records are not linked. Belgium has made use of modern encryption methods and local storage to protect privacy and prevent data-sharing, an approach opposite to the Home Office's. The UK scheme is closest to those of some Middle Eastern countries and of the People's Republic of China – though the latter has largely given up on biometrics.

The Government has not made a case. There is no evidence the system will produce the stated benefits. Less liberty does not imply greater security

Terrorism

ID does not establish intention. Competent criminals and terrorists will be able to subvert the identity system. Random outrages by individuals can't be stopped. Ministers

agree that ID cards will not prevent atrocities. A blank assertion that the department would find it helpful is not an argument that would be entertained for fundamental change in any other sphere of government but national security. Where is the evidence? Research suggests there is no link between the use of identity cards and the prevalence of terrorism, and in no instance has the presence of an identity card system been shown a significant deterrent to terrorist activity. Experts attest that ID unjustifiably presumed secure actually diminishes security.

Illegal immigration and working

People will still enter Britain using foreign documents – genuine or forged – and ID cards offer no more deterrent to people smugglers than passports and visas. Employers already face substantial penalties for failing to obtain proof of entitlement to work, yet there are only a handful of prosecutions a year.

Benefit fraud and abuse of public services

Identity is 'only a tiny part of the problem in the benefit system'. Figures for claims under false identity are estimated at £50 million (2.5%) of an (estimated) £2 billion per year in fraudulent claims.

'Identity fraud'

Both Australia and the USA have far worse problems of identity theft than Britain, precisely because of

general reliance on a single reference source. Costs usually cited for identity-related crime here include much fraud not susceptible to an ID system. Nominally 'secure', trusted, ID is more useful to the fraudster. The Home Office has not explained how it will stop registration by identity thieves in the personae of innocent others. Coherent collection of all sensitive personal data by government, and its easy transmission between departments, will create vast new opportunities for data-theft.

Overcomplicated, unproven technology

Computer system

IT providers find that identity systems work best when limited in design. The Home Office scheme combines untested technologies on an unparalleled scale. Its many inchoate purposes create innumerable points for failure. The government record with computer projects is poor, and the ID system is likely to end up a broken mess.

Biometrics

Not all biometrics will work for all people. Plenty are missing digits, or eyes, or have physical conditions that render one or more biometrics unstable or hard to read. All systems have error. Deployment on a vast scale, with variably trained operators and variably maintained and calibrated equipment, will produce vast numbers of mismatches, leading to potentially gross inconvenience to millions.

Identity cards will cost money that could be better spent

No ceiling

The Government has not ventured figures for the cost to the country as whole of the identity management scheme. That makes evaluation difficult. Civil Service IT experience suggests current projections are likely to be seriously underestimated. Home Office figures are for internal costs only, and have risen sharply – where they are not utterly obscure. Industry estimates suggest that public and private sector compliance costs could easily be double whatever is spent centrally.

Opportunity costs

The Government has not even tried

to show that national ID management will be more cost-effective than less spectacular alternative, targeted, solutions to the same problems (whether tried and tested or novel). We are to trust to luck that it is.

Taxpayer pain

Even at current Home Office estimates, the additional tax burden of setting up the scheme will be of the order of £200 per person. The direct cost to individuals (of a combined passport and ID card package) is quoted as £93. The impact on other departmental and local authority budgets is unknown. The scope and impact of arbitrary penalties would make speed cameras trivial by comparison.

Unchecked executive powers
Broad delegated power

The Home Office seeks wide discretion over the future shape of the scheme. There are more than 30 types of regulatory power for future Secretaries of State that would change the functions and content of the system ad lib. The scope, application and possible extension are extra-parliamentary decisions, even if nominally subject to approval.

Presumption of accuracy

Data entered onto the National Identity Register (NIR) is arbitrarily presumed to be accurate, and the Home Secretary made a judge of accuracy of information provided to him. Meanwhile, the Home Office gets the power to enter information without informing the individual. But there's no duty to ensure that such data is accurate, or criterion of accuracy. Personal identity is implicitly made wholly subject to state control.

Compulsion by stealth

Even during the so-called 'voluntary phase', the Home Secretary can add any person to the Register without their consent, and categories of individuals might be compelled selectively to register using powers under any future legislation. Anyone newly applying for a passport or other 'designated document', or renewing an existing one, will automatically have to be interviewed and submit all required details. This is less a phased introduction than a clandestine one. There is to be no choice. And the

minimum of notice to the public about the change in the handling of their registrable information.

Limited oversight

As proposed, the National Identity Scheme Commissioner would have very limited powers and is excluded from considering a number of key issues. He does not even report directly to Parliament. The reliance on administrative penalties means severe punishments may be inflicted without judicial process. The onus is on the individual to seek relief from the courts, at a civil standard of proof. Those who most require the protection of a fair trial are the least likely to be able to resort to legal action.

The scheme makes myriad small errors potentially catastrophic

---

Individuals managed by executive order

Without reference to the courts or any appeals process, the Home Secretary may cancel or require surrender of an identity card, without a right of appeal, at any time. Given that the object of the scheme is that an ID card will be eventually required to exercise any ordinary civil function, this amounts to granting the Home Secretary the power of civic life and death.

The National Identity Register creates specific new threats to individuals
Discrimination – no guarantees

There have been vapid 'assurances' made to some minority groups. That underlines the potential for threat. The system offers a ready-made police-state tool for a future government less trustworthy than the current one. A Home Secretary could create classifications of individuals to be registered as he sees fit, introducing onerous duties backed by severe penalties for fractions of the population. Religious or ethnic affiliation, for example, could be added to the Register by regulation – or

be inferred by cross-referencing other information using a National Identity Register Number or associated data.
'Papers, please'

ID cards in practice would provide a pretext for those in authority – public or private – to question individuals who stand out for reasons of personal appearance or demeanour. This is likely to exacerbate divisions in society. The Chairman of the Bar Council has asked, 'is there not a great risk that those who feel at the margins of society – the somewhat disaffected – will be driven into the arms of extremists?'

Third party abuse

The requirement that all those registered notify all changes in details risks creating the means of tracking and persecution through improper use of the database. A variety of persons have good reason to conceal their identity and whereabouts; for example: those fleeing domestic abuse; victims of 'honour' crimes; witnesses in criminal cases; those at risk of kidnapping; undercover investigators; refugees from oppressive regimes overseas; those pursued by the press; those who may be terrorist targets. The seizure of ID cards (like benefit-books and passports now) will become a means for extortion by gangsters.

Lost identity, becoming an unperson

By making ordinary life dependent on the reliability of a complex administrative system, the scheme makes myriad small errors potentially catastrophic. There's no hint from the government how it will deal with inevitably large numbers of mis-identifications and errors, or deliberate attacks on or corruption of what would become a critical piece of national infrastructure. A failure in any part of the system at a check might deny a person access to his or her rights or property or to public services, with no immediate solution or redress – 'license to live' withdrawn.

⇨ The above information is reprinted with kind permission from the NO2ID campaign. Visit www.no2id.net for more information.
© The NO2ID campaign

Councils ordered to stop snooping on residents

Councils will be ordered to stop spying on local residents amid Government concerns over the continuing creep of the surveillance state

By Rosa Prince

Ministers from the Department of Communities and the Home Office have undertaken a thorough review of official surveillance powers, some of which are open to public bodies such as local authorities, the NHS and even the Coastguard.

Ministers believe that while surveillance including covert cameras is sometimes necessary to detect offences such as fraud, it must only be used as a last resort and in the most serious cases

The review was triggered by ministers' concerns that incidents where council staff were found putting microchips into residents' dustbins and tailing parents to school had eroded public support for the entire enforcement system.

Two-thirds of councils have taken up the snooping powers open to them under the Regulation of Investigative Powers Act since its introduction in 2000.

Ministers believe that while surveillance including covert cameras is sometimes necessary to detect offences such as fraud, it must only be used as a last resort and in the most serious cases.

They plan to issue guidance and set strict new limits to ensure that in future the RIPA powers are not used to tackle minor infringements of the law or local regulations.

John Healey, Local Government Minster, said: 'My main concern is to tighten up the operation of the system so it can command the public confidence that is needed.

'Councils do need these powers, but they need to use them only when it is necessary and proportionate, and only if the information cannot be found another way. They should not be used lightly, because their use is a serious business.'

A number of councils have been accused of snooping since the introduction of RIPA, often for putting microchips in rubbish bins to discover if items had been thrown away which should have been put out to be recycled.

Earlier this year, Poole Council in Dorset defended its decision to tail three families as they walked with their children, to find out whether they had given a false address in order to appear within the catchment area of a popular school.

Under the new guidelines council staff will be warned that they should not generally use surveillance to check domestic waste or to detect low grade offending such as dog fouling or the misuse of disabled driver badges.

Instead, RIPA powers should be limited to serious cases, such as loan sharks, fly-tippers and rogue traders.

In Wolverhampton recently, covert cameras were used to catch fly-tippers who had vandalised CCTV, leading to the prosecution of an offender who had dumped 300 tyres, while Birmingham Council was able to catch 150 loan sharks using communications surveillance.

Mr Healey said: 'As well as being a matter of principle, the problem with using RIPA too freely is that every time one of these cases comes to light it leads to serious criminals like loan sharks and rogue traders rubbing their hands together.

'They know that growing public concern means councils are more reluctant to use the powers that they should quite rightly be deploying against proper crooks.

'As long as councils and other public bodies understand that they should be adopted only as a last resort, then we encourage their use in the right circumstances.

'These are heavy duty powers and they are needed to detect heavy duty crimes in cases were evidence cannot be gathered in any other way.'
24 September 2008

⇨ The above information is reprinted with kind permission from RINF. Visit http://rinf.com for more information.

© RINF

Councils have been accused of misusing surveillance powers designed to combat terrorism for petty snooping

How councils are using surveillance

Information from the Press Association

Councils across Britain are routinely using the Regulation of Investigatory Powers Act (RIPA) to snoop on dog foulers, litterbugs and illegal parkers.

In April, the Press Association surveyed nearly 100 councils and discovered the legislation was used to find out about people who let their dog foul (at least seven cases), breaches of planning law (one case), animal welfare (one case), littering (at least one case) and even the misuse of a disabled parking badge (one case).

The research took place to find the extent of the 'surveillance Britain' after a family in Poole in Dorset were tracked covertly for nearly three weeks to check they lived in a school catchment area.

The same council has made similar checks on two other families in the last year under RIPA and defended its actions by saying the cases were treated as potential criminal activity, which allowed it to spy under the law.

Poole council also snooped on fishermen to see whether they were illegally catching shellfish.

In the survey the large majority of the surveillance was used to combat rogue traders, benefit fraud, counterfeit goods and antisocial behaviour like noise nuisance and criminal damage.

Under RIPA, councils can conduct surveillance if they suspect criminal activity, they can also ask for subscriber details of Internet and telephone bills but they cannot tap phones or intercept emails.

But the interpretation of what is criminal activity has led to some debate.

Four councils – Derby City, Bolton, Gateshead and Hartlepool – used surveillance to investigate dog fouling, with Bolton also using the act to find out about littering, the research found.

Kensington and Chelsea conducted surveillance in regard to the misuse of a disabled parking badge.

Liverpool city council used it for one case of a false claim for damages investigation.

Denbighshire county council used surveillance for one animal welfare investigation and Conwy council had one case where it used the law to spy on someone who was working while off sick.

In other areas, the surveillance law was used by Redcar and Cleveland for a food hygiene investigation (one case) and Newcastle used it for one case of 'car parking surveillance re suspected contraventions of parking orders'.
23 June 2008

© *The Press Association*

Council leaders respond to 'snooping' allegations

Information from the Local Government Association

Responding to the findings of a Press Association Freedom of Information Inquiry which has detailed the number of times councils have used the Regulation of Investigatory Powers Act (RIPA), Sir Simon Milton, Chairman of the Local Government Association, said:

'Councils are committed to putting local people first and will use every weapon in their arsenal to catch the rogue traders, doorstep criminals and scam artists who cheat the taxpayer and prey on the vulnerable and the elderly.

'Councils are using these powers to respond to residents' complaints about rip-off merchants, fly-tippers and benefit fraudsters. Without these powers councils would not be able to provide the same level of reassurance and protection local people demand and deserve.

'It's wrong to suggest that these are specifically anti-terror powers. What this legislation actually does is control how a number of public bodies, including councils, carry out surveillance to tackle crime. There are strict rules to protect people from unnecessary intrusion and whenever a council applies to use these powers they must prove that it is both necessary and proportionate to the crime being investigated.

'There needs to be a national debate about how we can get the balance right between responding to the needs of local people who are worried about crime, disorder and antisocial behaviour and the need to make sure people's privacy is protected.

'We are working closely with the government, police chiefs and the surveillance commissioners to clarify some of the details of the legislation and make sure it is clear when and how surveillance should be used. We are also working on developing training for councils on the use of these powers to make sure they know exactly when it is appropriate to use them.'
28 April 2008

⇨ The above information is reprinted with kind permission from the Local Government Association. Visit www.lga.gov.uk for more information.

© *Local Government Association*

CCTV

A briefing from politics.co.uk

What is CCTV?

'CCTV' stands for closed circuit television.

CCTV is used for a number of monitoring and surveillance purposes, but is mainly used for security purposes.

CCTV involves the use of an unmanned, remotely mounted video camera system, transmitting live pictures back to a television screen where developments can be monitored and recorded.

Background

CCTV was first developed in the late 1970s and was initially confined to high-risk security targets, such as banks.

The units were expensive and picture quality was poor for a long time, with the vague grainy silhouettes of fugitives attracting some public derision when broadcast on programmes such as *Crimewatch*.

Since then, the quality of CCTV has improved dramatically and the use of CCTV has risen exponentially, with shops and the police the primary consumers of the technology.

Modern CCTV cameras are now capable of remote operation and produce high-resolution colour picture quality. CCTV has come so far that it is now capable of recognising individual car number plates and recording them on central databases. The congestion-charging scheme introduced in London in 2003 is an example of the advancing potential of CCTV technology.

Controversies

The development of CCTV was felt by many to be a major breakthrough in crime prevention. It forms a major part of crime prevention strategy in the UK and is often used as important evidence in court trials and in the identification of suspects. CCTV may have other deterrence and safety-related benefits, although these are debated.

However, the proliferation of CCTV cameras in public places has led to some unease about the erosion of civil liberties and individual human rights, along with warnings of an Orwellian 'Big Brother' culture.

Critics of CCTV say that constant CCTV surveillance of public places is intrusive and a breach of privacy. What is done with recorded CCTV footage is also a matter of some controversy.

This complaint is illustrated by the case of Geoffrey Peck, who was 'caught' on CCTV in 1995 attempting to commit suicide on Brentford town centre High Street. The footage was then widely disseminated to the public at large, without his consent. In 2003, the European Court of Human Rights found that, although Mr Peck was in a 'public' place he was still entitled to some privacy and that it was not foreseeable for him to have expected so much public exposure.

Therefore, the Court considered the use of the material and the lack of remedial relief under UK law to be a breach of Article Eight of the European Convention on Human Rights, the right to respect for family and private life, and the UK was ordered to pay compensation to Mr Peck.

The case highlighted potential gaps in the UK's protection of individual privacy and helped influence MPs' calls for the introduction of a free-standing privacy law in 2003.

Statistics

⇨ In 1990, there were three town centre schemes in the UK with approximately 100 cameras.

⇨ In 1994, there were 16 town centre schemes with approximately 400 cameras.

⇨ In 1997, there were 167 schemes with approximately 5,238 cameras.

⇨ By the end of 2002, there were an estimated 500 systems with 40,000 cameras.

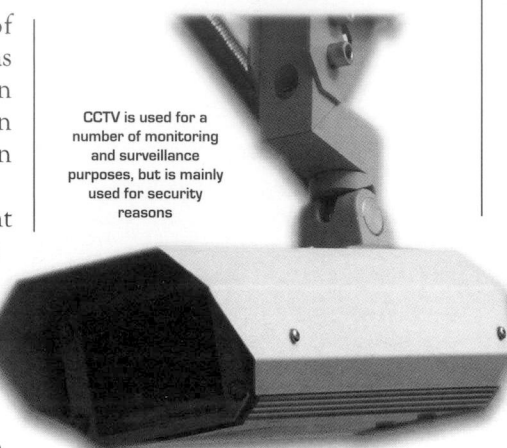

CCTV is used for a number of monitoring and surveillance purposes, but is mainly used for security reasons

⇨ Between 1999 and 2003 the Home Office pledged £170 million for CCTV schemes.
(*Source: NACRO report 'To CCTV or not to CCTV?', 2002*)

Quotes

'Three-quarters of the Home Office Crime Prevention budget was spent on CCTV between 1996 and 1998, yet a comprehensive review has revealed the overall reduction in crime was only five per cent. A parallel systematic review carried out by the Home Office that looked at street lighting, however, found a highly significant reduction in crime of twenty per cent.'
NACRO, *'To CCTV or not to CCTV?'*, 2002

'CCTV has a broadly positive reception from members of the general public. Levels of concern are not high and CCTV is assumed to be effective in crime control. However, public acceptance is based on limited, and partly inaccurate knowledge of the functions and capabilities of CCTV systems in public places.'
Home Office report, 'CCTV in Public Places', 1991

'Big Brother is Watching You.'
George Orwell, '1984', 1948

⇨ The above information is reprinted with kind permission from politics.co.uk. Visit www.politics. co.uk for more information.
© *Adfero*

CCTV and crime prevention

Britain's multi-billion-pound CCTV network 'an utter fiasco which has failed to cut crime'

By Craig Brown

Britain's network of CCTV cameras has been branded 'an utter fiasco' for failing to cut crime, despite billions of pounds being spent on it.

Detective Chief Inspector Mick Neville, who is in charge of closed-circuit television for the Metropolitan Police Force, claimed only 3 per cent of the capital's street robberies are solved using security camera footage and criminals are not afraid of being caught on film.

The UK has the highest level of camera surveillance in the world, according to civil liberty groups and security experts, with an estimated 4.2 million CCTV cameras on buildings, shops, roads and stations.

Mr Neville told the Security Document World Conference in London: 'CCTV was originally seen as a preventative measure. Billions of pounds has been spent on kit, but no thought has gone into how the police are going to use the images and how they will be used in court.

'It's been an utter fiasco.'

His comments echo a government report last October which said most CCTV footage is not of high enough quality to help police identify offenders, with many cameras focused on enforcing bus lanes as well as stopping crime.

The report said anecdotal evidence suggests more than 80 per cent of CCTV images supplied to the police are not up to scratch.

Mr Neville, who is head of the Metropolitan Police's division on visual images, identifications and detection, is now leading an initiative to increase conviction rates from CCTV.

He aims to set up a database of images to track down offenders and to put pictures of suspects in crimes such as muggings and rape on the Internet.

Mr Neville said the work 'has to be balanced against any Big Brother concerns, with safeguards'.

Work is under way to ascertain whether software can be developed to perform automated searches for suspects on footage, while Mr Neville said officers needed more training on using CCTV, with many being put off because 'it's hard work'.

Last night, a spokesman for the Metropolitan Police said the force 'does not consider that CCTV has failed'.

He added: 'CCTV is an important tool in protecting the public both as a deterrent and in the investigation of a wide range of crime, from minor offences to terrorism.'

Assistant Chief Constable John Pollock, of the Association of Chief Police Officers in Scotland (Acpos), also gave his support for CCTV.

He said: 'Acpos fully supports the use of CCTV and stresses its important role both in the prevention and detection of crime in protecting our communities.

'Recently reported comments on the effectiveness of CCTV paint a view not reflected by experience in Scotland, where police forces actively use evidence gathered by CCTV whenever possible.'

A spokeswoman for the Scottish Government said it would continue to use the system in crime prevention.

She said: 'This government is committed to making our communities safer by tackling crime and the fear of crime.

'Clearly, technology such as CCTV systems can have a role to play in helping to achieve this, and is a tool used by the police to investigate crime, gather intelligence about problem areas, monitor crowds and tackle antisocial behaviour.

'We are currently working on research to give better information on the coverage and use of CCTV in our communities.'

The spokeswoman added that the government was working to put more than 1,000 additional police officers on the streets to tackle the drink, drugs and deprivation which are the underlying causes of crime.

The Scottish Government's CCTV review is due to be completed in July. It will examine how many cameras are in use and the system's effectiveness in deterrence, detection and evidence gathering.

Surveillance system with wartime roots

Though considered a phenomenon of the modern age, the origins of CCTV cameras can be traced to the Second World War.

They were first developed to allow German engineers to observe the launch of V2 rockets.

In the UK, CCTV, though initially used for security by banks, was developed on a larger scale in response to IRA bombings. Trial programmes carried out by the government during the early 1990s led to the report 'CCTV: Looking Out For You', which paved the way for the massive increase in the number of CCTV systems installed.

The proliferation of cameras has led to claims that public civil liberties are at risk. However, authorities claim they are an effective tool in fighting and deterring crime.

7 May 2008

Predicting crime with CCTV

Portsmouth to trial crime-predicting CCTV cameras

The city of Portsmouth will become the first in the UK to get a taste of a new generation of smart CCTV cameras which can alert authorities if they detect any suspicious behaviour, prompting some to label them as 'Minority Report' cameras in reference to the 2002 sci-fi movie featuring Tom Cruise.

The security system is already in use in New York and other cities across the Atlantic and works by analysing how vehicles and people behave using a number of variables like speed. But the human operator still has the last word as whether to inform the authorities or not.

The system is said to allow the human operators to concentrate on the 'most interesting' information as the software filters out 'all the boring ones', which in effect means that operators could be given the task to monitor even more CCTVs.

And Portsmouth's Council Tax payers will not pay a single penny for it after Smart CCTV, the company behind the product, gave it free to the city in a bid to raise its profile. 4.2 million cameras are currently in use in the country and Portsmouth plans to equip up to 600 existing CCTV cameras with the new technology after the initial trial was a success.

In a near future, human controllers might even be removed from the equation if the service is crowdsourced (piggy-backing on neighbourhood watch schemes) or if advanced artificial intelligence is used together with face recognition systems.

'Although we are a long way off *Minority Report*, it is a step closer, It is able to alert the operator to something that might be interesting such as a guy hanging around or somebody running,' said Nick Hewitson, MD of Smart CCTV... *Minority Report* is much closer, indeed.
29 November 2008

⇨ Information reprinted with kind permission from ITProPortal.com.
© *Net Communities*

CCTV and sound recording

CCTV operators must not record conversations, says new guidance

Closed-circuit television (CCTV) system operators would need exceptional justification for recording sound as well as video, the Information Commissioner's Office (ICO) has warned.

In a newly revised CCTV code of practice the ICO said that sound recording is intrusive and unnecessary in most circumstances, and that the use of sound recording could undermine any public support there is for CCTV.

The UK has more CCTV cameras than any other country in the world according to the ICO. There are an estimated 4.5 million cameras in the country, recording the average person 300 times a day, according to some estimates.

The ICO has raised concerns about a trend for attaching microphones and sound recording equipment to cameras.

'CCTV must not be used to record conversations between members of the public as this is highly intrusive and unlikely to be justified,' said the new guidance. 'You should choose a system without this facility if possible. If your system comes equipped with a sound recording facility then you should turn this off or disable it in some other way.'

The ICO said that there are limited circumstances in which audio could be used, such as help systems where a person can initiate a conversation with an operator. But some things should never be recorded, it said. 'Conversations must not be recorded, and operators should not listen in.' said the guidance. 'In the limited circumstances where audio recording is justified, signs must make it very clear that audio recording is being or may be carried out.'

Assistant commissioner at the ICO Jonathan Bamford said that organisations must be careful in their use of cameras and recording equipment. '[CCTV] can be extremely intrusive, monitoring ordinary individuals as they go about their day-to-day business,' he said. 'It is essential that organisations and businesses use CCTV responsibly in order to maintain public trust and confidence in the use of CCTV and to prevent its use becoming increasingly viewed as part of the surveillance society.'

The ICO conducted a consultation exercise on the new guidance and has just published the updated code of practice.

It also conducted research into the attitudes of the public to audio recording. It said that it found seven out of 10 people surveyed were opposed to the use of audio recording as part of CCTV systems. It also found that almost half of those surveyed were not aware that the use of CCTV is covered by the Data Protection Act, one of the laws which the ICO is charged with enforcing.

The introduction of new rules may not do enough to make CCTV systems illegal. CCTV compliance consultant Bernie Brooks told OUT-LAW Radio last year that in his experience 95% of systems were operating outside of existing laws regarding notification of the collection of information and registering with the ICO.

'I would say that 95% are non-compliant in one way, shape, form or another with the [Data Protection] Act,' he said. 'Obviously that's quite a worrying thing. If the system is non-compliant it could invalidate the usefulness of the evidence in a court of law.'

29 January 2008

CCTV in schools

85% of teachers have CCTV in their schools and nearly 25% worry about hidden cameras – ATL

Eighty-five per cent of teachers say that they have CCTV in their schools and nearly a quarter worry about hidden cameras within their building. In the majority of cases, according to members of the Association of Teachers and Lecturers (ATL), the surveillance cameras are covering the school grounds and entrances to the school, but nearly 10 per cent say CCTV is operating in the toilets.

Who's watching? 85% of teachers say they have CCTV cameras installed in their schools

These are the key findings in a preliminary survey of teachers and lecturers working in both independent and state schools throughout the UK. An ATL working group is looking into the use of CCTV in schools and colleges, and will produce best practice guidance at the end of the year.

According to the survey, 98 per cent of teachers say that CCTV is primarily used for security and monitoring vandalism around the building. However, over half of the teachers reported that the surveillance is also present inside the school to monitor the behaviour of the pupils within school hours.

Nearly a quarter of teachers surveyed said they were worried about hidden cameras within their school environments. A teacher in a state school expressed a common view that 'regular use of cameras in class would be intimidating'.

Dr Mary Bousted, general secretary of ATL, commented: 'No one really knows enough about the use of CCTV in schools – it's a very new issue. We have set up a working group to look into the use of CCTV and produce ATL guidelines on best practice for schools and colleges throughout the UK.

'Certainly we would want staff to be involved in decisions about the use of CCTV in schools, and strict safeguards for its use. Although surveillance in schools can have some positive outcomes, such as discouraging vandalism and violence, we think there are some instances where it should be strictly controlled.'

The vast majority of teachers questioned believed that CCTV made them feel safer within their school environment. Tonia Matthews, teacher at Trinity secondary school in West Berkshire, says that 'students feel secure to know if there has been an incident, i.e. bullying, we can then go back and look at what happened.' Another member, Elaine Brown, from Portchester secondary school in Bournemouth, reinforces this belief by saying that the use of CCTV in her school has 'helped to reduce bullying considerably'. However, over half of the teachers involved in the survey thought the presence of CCTV cameras would not result in students behaving any differently.

Over 50 per cent of the teachers surveyed admit to concerns about the use of CCTV around their schools. A teacher from a special school in Northamptonshire states that she objects to 'general monitoring of staff' and is also 'not sure that all management can be trusted to just use it with notification and in agreement for CPD [Continuing Professional Development]'.

Members also say there are circumstances where they would prefer the surveillance to be disabled – such as 'in the classroom, where you would always feel like you were being watched and judged'.

Nearly two-thirds of teachers surveyed do not know what security measures their school has for use of CCTV within their schools, and are not sure about the policies for restricting the use of surveillance data. One of the problems caused by this lack of knowledge is noted by Louise Davies, a teacher from a secondary school in Brighton, who stated that 'where there is not a high level of trust, staff may have concerns that evidence may be gathered against them'.

However, 61 per cent of teachers said that CCTV can have positive uses. A teacher in an independent school stated that surveillance within the school building has 'reduced the level of abuse issues against staff and students'; and another added that 'in the classroom, it can be a useful tool for professional development'. Despite this, the general consensus from the survey is that classroom surveillance is an invasion of privacy, disrupts education and 'should not be allowed in the classroom, where you would always feel like you were being watched and judged'.

18 August 2008

Satellite surveillance

Information from Privacy International

Developments in satellite surveillance (also called 'remote sensing') during the last decade have embraced features similar to those of more conventional visual surveillance. Satellite resolution has constantly improved since the end of the Cold War, largely due to efforts by companies such as EarthWatch, Motorola and Boeing. These companies have invested billions of dollars to create satellites capable of mapping even the most minute detail on the face of the earth.

The use of commercial satellite imagery by governments has increased substantially in recent years

The use of commercial satellite imagery by governments has increased substantially in recent years. Images obtained through commercial satellites were key in aiding US military forces carrying out Operation Iraqi Freedom. The US Commercial Remote Sensing Space Policy, signed in 2003, ordered all federal government agencies to utilize commercial satellite imagery and encouraged development of a strong US remote sensing industry. Space Imaging (now part of Geo-Eye) and DigitalGlobe are the two major players in the commercial satellite industry, collecting thousands of square kilometres of imagery each day. Both companies are the recipients of substantial contracts with the US government for images from their satellites.

Space Imaging was the first to launch one of the new generation high-resolution satellites, the IKONOS, in September 1999. ORBIMAGE acquired Space Imaging in 2006 to form GeoEye, the world's largest commercial remote sensing company. Its parabolic lens can recognise objects as small as one metre (3.28 feet) anywhere on earth and, according to the company, viewers can see individual trees, automobiles, road networks, and houses. Collecting data at a rate of over 2,000 square kilometres (772 square miles) per minute, the volume of imagery provided by this satellite is staggering. Considered the grandfather of commercial satellites, IKONOS is used by a number of industries in addition to government. Public interest groups are also using the information to show images of nuclear testing by countries and even images of secret United States bases such as Area 51 in Nevada. GeoEye's latest prototype, the GeoEye-1, is due to be launched at the end of 2007. Touted as the world's highest resolution commercial Earth-imaging satellite, the GeoEye-1 will be able to precisely locate an object to within 3 metres of its true location on the surface of the Earth, and is able to recognise objects as small as 0.41 metres. The satellite will be able to collect up to 700,000 square kilometres of imagery per day. GeoEye-1 will be able to revisit any point on Earth once every three days or sooner.

In 2001, DigitalGlobe launched the satellite QuickBird, which provides images as small as two feet (0.61 metres). DigitalGlobe is currently working on improving resolution and collection capacity with their next-generation WorldView 1 satellite, scheduled to launch in mid-2007, and its WorldView 2 satellite, anticipated to launch in late 2008.

While governments are increasingly relying on commercial satellite technology, private companies are raising public awareness by providing access to images through the Internet. Upon acquisition of the satellite image firm, Keyhole, in October 2004, Google Inc. combined satellite imagery, maps and its popular search engine to create Google Earth. Google Earth is a free download that allows users to view a map in satellite form by simply entering an address or executing a search. The service is still in the early stages, and the level of resolution varies from distant aerial photographs to street level, depending on the area. For an additional fee, the company offers two upgraded versions of Google Earth, incorporating Global Positioning System (GPS) technology and data import capability for more advanced application. The satellite option was initially offered through Google's

"shopping trolley 25 metres east... and by the way, your driveway needs sweeping!"

Internet mapping service, Google Maps, but in a more limited form. Other companies, such as Microsoft, also offer satellite imagery through various websites. On 25 May 2007, Google released Street View, a new feature of Google Maps that provides 360-degree panoramic street-level views of New York City, San Francisco, Miami, Denver, Las Vegas, Orlando, San Diego, Los Angeles, Houston, and their surrounding metropolitan areas. The service has raised some privacy objections as Street View displays detailed images of home interiors as well as images of shelters and clinics.

Integration of existing satellite images with ground-based Geographic Information System (GIS) databases have produced interactive maps available for widespread use. GIS technology allows users to link detailed data on human activity to mapping software. Information ranging from census data to crime statistics may be incorporated into these maps. Because there is no limit to the types of information that can be linked to satellite imagery, the implications of this technology are far-reaching. Were personal information integrated into such a map, simply double-clicking on a satellite image of an urban area could reveal precise details about the occupants of a particular house. The 'Open Skies' policy accepted worldwide means that there are few restrictions of the use of the technology.

Despite these advances, private companies have a distance to go before they catch up with governments. Experts estimate that the current generation of secret spy satellites, such as the Ikon/Keyhole-12, can recognise objects as small as ten centimetres (approximately four inches) across and some analysts say that it can image a licence plate. The aeroplane manufacturer Boeing is currently fulfilling a 10-year contract with the United States government for a Future Imagery Architecture (FIA) to replace the KH satellites and the ground infrastructure. The FIA is based on a constellation of new satellites that are smaller, less expensive, and placed in orbit to allow for real-time surveillance of battlefields and other targets.

Government use of satellites is extensive, ranging from homeland security operations to agricultural analysis. For example, the United Nations (UN) Office on Drugs and Crime uses IKONOS imagery to assess the illegal drug trade in Afghanistan, Laos, Myanmar, and Bolivia. By analysing satellite images, the UN is able to assess the level of production of illicit crops such as heroin and cocaine, and estimate the portion of the drug trade attributable to these nations.

Following the 11 September 2001 terrorist attacks on the United States, the US National Geospatial Intelligence Agency (NGA) began focusing its observation internally rather than abroad. Prior to the attacks, domestic US satellite surveillance most often involved natural disaster relief. Although laws limit the use of intelligence resources to issues of national security, the NGA admits to the existence of grey areas in which aiding the FBI in criminal investigations is common practice. In 2004, the NGA signed a sharing agreement with the National Security Administration that allows 'horizontal integration' between the two agencies, defined as 'working together from start to finish, using NGA's "eyes" and NSA "ears".' Using a combination of wire-tap surveillance and satellite imagery obtained from unmanned aerial vehicles, intelligence analysts have tracked suspected terrorists or insurgents in Iraq in real time.

GPS developments

Development of the European satellite system, Galileo, will likely enhance surveillance technology. The first satellite launched at the end of 2005, and the system should be fully operational by 2010. Galileo will be fully interoperable with GPS and, when used in conjunction, will offer much greater reliability and an expected accuracy of close to one metre.

Use of GPS is becoming increasingly common, as the technology finds its way into consumer wireless devices such as cellular phones, personal data assistants, and car navigation systems. Although GPS provides convenient

Governments are increasingly using satellite images for military surveillance

navigational assistance, the ability for others to track users raises serious concerns. A number of relatively inexpensive devices, advertising the ability to covertly monitor the movements of individuals, are currently on the market.

Employer use of GPS to monitor their workforce is also on the rise. The number of trackers installed on fleet vehicles in the US is expected to exceed 1.3 million by 2005. Some companies require employees to carry GPS-enabled cell phones to allow for tracking on the job. Employers cite legitimate purposes for such monitoring but the lack of clear standards governing this practice leaves the potential for abuse wide open.

New York taxi drivers have promised to go on strike in September 2007 unless the city halts plans to install GPS technology in the city's 13,000 cabs by early 2008. Members of the New York Taxi Workers' Alliance, which represents about 8,400 drivers, are worried that their bosses will track their whereabouts even when they are off-duty. Australian company Telstra could face a police investigation following a report that claims that workers were monitored illegally by surveillance devices in their vehicles. It is a criminal act in Victoria to install tracking devices in vehicles without permission from the workers.
18 December 2007

⇨ The above information is re-printed with kind permission from Privacy International. Visit www. privacyinternational.org for more information.

© Privacy International

Privacy and the media

Information from Liberty

One area where the rights under Article 8 of the Convention have had a significant effect is in relation to the media. The laws of breach of confidence, trespass, nuisance, surveillance, harassment etc., apply equally to the media and you may be able to bring actions against the media where they have infringed those laws. Libel may restrict some intrusions on private life but only if the words are defamatory in that they discredit the individual or lower him or her in the estimation of others. In reality, however, actions for libel are of limited use as a means of protecting against intrusions of privacy. If the words relate to a private matter but are substantially true, then an action for libel is likely to be successfully defended. Moreover, public funding is not available for libel actions so they are less useful to an individual of limited means.

In practice, it has often been very difficult to control the worst excesses of the media and flagrant breaches of the rights of privacy of individuals have been allowed to go on without redress. This does not simply apply to celebrities or royalty. In many cases, the media have significantly intruded upon the rights of unknown individuals who have become famous or, more usually, infamous as a result.

In the absence of any right to privacy as such, lawyers have had to resort to strange suits to try and prevent invasions of privacy. In this respect, actions for malicious falsehood were on the rise. In theory, public funding for actions of this type is available. Malicious falsehood was notoriously used as a cause of action against a newspaper which photographed and interviewed a famous actor who was recovering in hospital from brain surgery at a time when he was not in a fit state to consent to such an interview. The court dealing with the claim recognised that the remarks which the patient had made were wrongly portrayed as part of a voluntary and exclusive interview.

In practice, it has often been very difficult to control the worst excesses of the media and flagrant breaches of the rights of privacy of individuals have been allowed to go on without redress

---

However, the newspaper got round this problem by publishing a statement that the interview was not voluntary or exclusive. This did not enable the real mischief, the invasion of the actor's privacy at a time when he was most vulnerable and sensitive, to be dealt with and the courts have been criticised for failing to develop the law so as to protect people in positions such as this. The ingredients for an action in malicious falsehood are also difficult to establish. The victim must show that the words are false, that they were published maliciously and that they have either caused financial loss or, in some cases, were likely to cause such loss.

Copyright can also be used as a way of preventing publication of private papers or pictures, but working out who owns copyright – and who is therefore the right person to bring an action – can be a complicated matter. Additional protection is given to a person who commissions photographs for private or domestic purposes. Even if the photographer owns copyright, that person can prevent their publication.

It is these inadequacies that may be resolved by the incorporation of Article 8. It is clear from the recent cases involving press intrusion that the courts are prepared to give effect to the rights under Article 8 by expanding the existing cause of action of breach of confidence.

The courts are also themselves under an obligation to act compatibly with Article 8. Although there is no requirement on private individuals or companies – such as journalists and newspapers – to act compatibly with Article 8, the courts may be increasingly willing to develop the common law so as to provide proper protection for privacy. A recent decision from the House of Lords suggests that there is continued reluctance to recognise a new right to privacy and the Government has rejected a recent Select Committee proposal urging the introduction of such a right. However, the development of existing causes of action will give much wider protection than was previously the case.

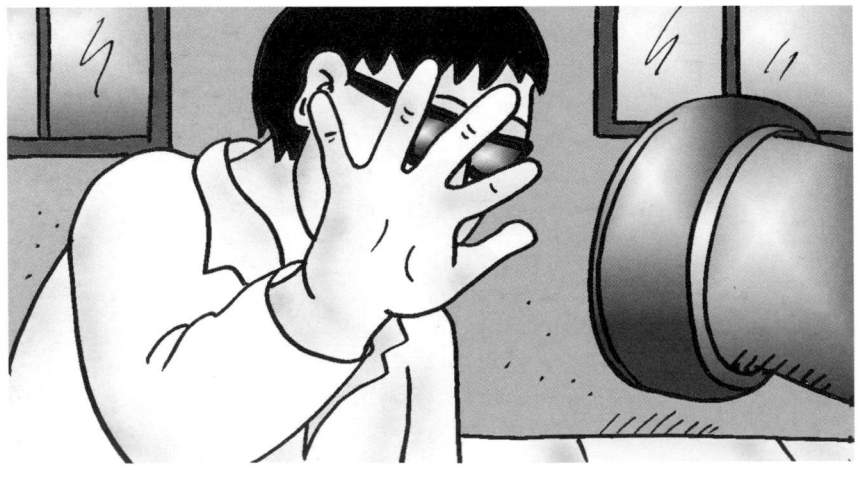

If you find yourself subject to unwanted press intrusion of this nature, then you should take legal advice in light of the latest developments of the law. This is a rapidly changing area. You may have a potential action for harassment under the Protection from Harassment Act. You may have an action for breach of confidence. You may have an action for breach of the Data Protection Act. You will also have the right to complain to either Ofcom, the Office of Communications, which regulates UK television and radio services, or the Press Complaints Commission. It is worth noting that the Press Complaints Commission is more likely to be responsive to privacy complaints involving 'intrusion into grief or shock', such as the publication of photographs taken at a funeral.

However, in every case, there will be a requirement to protect the right to freedom of expression and the right of the media to publish material of public interest. Each case will need to be carefully examined to see if the interests of freedom of expression outweigh your rights to private life. As a general rule, the courts will not intervene to protect you merely because the media are intending to publish material in a particularly lurid way. The courts are not there

to judge the taste of an article. They will be concerned with whether or not the material itself should be disclosed or published at all. Where you are seeking to prevent the media from publishing an article or putting out a programme, then the courts will apply the principles relating to injunctions which have been set out in the case involving the footballer Gary Flitcroft.

The court guidelines have been developed in consequence of the express provisions in the HRA dealing with claims for injunctions, which concern freedom of expression. Freedom of expression is, of course, a right which is also incorporated by the HRA through Article 10. In the context of the media, there will always be a tension on the one hand between protecting the right to freedom of expression and a free press with respect to rights of privacy on the other hand. Section 12 of the HRA deals expressly with this tension and makes it clear that any person seeking to restrain publication of material which might affect the exercise of freedom of expression will:

1 Take all practical steps to notify the intended publisher or show that there are compelling reasons why that person should not be notified.
2 Need to satisfy the court that

the underlying claim is likely to succeed at trial.
3 Need to deal with the court's obligation to have particular regard to the Convention right to freedom of expression; and
4 Where such material is journalistic, literary or artistic, will need to deal with the court's obligation to have particular regard to:
   (a) the extent to which the material is, or is about to become, available to the public and it would be in the interest of the public for it to be published;
   (b) any relevant privacy code.

This provision is designed to ensure that freedom of expression is not stifled by well-timed injunctions sought by persons at a time when the publisher of the material will not be able to deal with the application properly. However, it does not prevent you from seeking to obtain an injunction in circumstances where there has been an unjustifiable breach of your privacy and you have a good case of succeeding in litigation against the person responsible.

↪ The above information is reprinted with kind permission from Liberty. Visit www.yourrights.org.uk for more information.

© Liberty

Mosley's victory has a hollow ring for the rest of us

As a privacy law now seems inevitable, we must ensure it enshrines our freedoms, not erodes them still further

Max Mosley's victory in the High Court should be celebrated because it exposed the hypocrisy of the *News of the World*: its mean and suicidal decision to reduce payment to the call girl and main witness, Woman E, by more than half; the pomposity of editor Colin Myler, who insisted that he was motivated by public interest; and the blackmail, unreliability and inconsistencies of its reporter, Neville Thurlbeck.

By Henry Porter

Since the judgment, there has been much hand-wringing about the freedom of the press. Most of it is self-serving. The damage to the press has not been done by Mosley, or the law, but by the practices of the *News of the World*. The public-interest defence still remains, but because of the Mosley case, newspapers are now going to have to justify such

exposés under the chilly gaze of Mr Justice Eady and the accumulation of privacy law.

That's no bad thing, but my joy at the vanquishing of the *News of the World* is tempered by the knowledge that while our society haphazardly builds the law to protect privacy in this one limited sphere, we are busily destroying it in almost every other area.

In the last few weeks, we have learnt that government plans legislation to give the state access to every email, phone call, text message and Internet connection made in this country. The latest figures available show that under current laws, 500,000 requests were made during one year for private communications data. That figure is up on the previous two years by almost 30 per cent.

We also learnt that in the last year local councils have launched 10,000 operations to spy on members of the public who are thought to be guilty of minor misdemeanours such as fly-tipping, avoiding council tax or applying to a school out of their area. So, if I have got this right, a person who spends the afternoon with five call girls is now guaranteed privacy, but heaven protect him if he lets his dog foul the pavement. In the future, while Mr Mosley may visit Ms Whiplash in private, calls to his family could be monitored.

Sir Christopher Rose, the Chief Surveillance Commissioner, has attacked the growth in surveillance by saying that councils have 'a serious misunderstanding of the concept of proportionality'. I would extend that to the entire government, which is suffering several defensive illusions that suggest we are under attack from ever more violent crime and antisocial behaviour.

The figures tell the opposite. Nationally, violent crime has almost halved since the mid-nineties. Crime figures for the Metropolitan area show a fall of 14 per cent in knife crime and a similar amount in gun crime. There were 21 fewer murders (down from 175 to 154) and youth crime is down by 7 per cent.

The government - and to a lesser extent the public - is heedless of this steady downward trend and continues to argue for greater security and more intrusive measures. Few questioned the use by Staffordshire police of a remote-controlled spy drone to monitor crowds at the V Festival or bother to think of its potential use in spying on legitimate political demonstrations. 'How long will it be before someone gets Tasered from the air for dropping litter?' asked Noel Sharkey of Sheffield University. Just because the technology is available, we don't have to buy into it as a society.

The same is true of fingerprinting at schools. Chipping Campden School in Gloucestershire - you cannot think of a more idyllic, less threatening environment - has introduced biometric fingerprinting to stop bullying and truancy. A forensic attack on the policy by actor and director Chris Jury, whose son attends the school, shows that the system cannot stop bullying and will not stop truancy, because it logs pupils going into school but not leaving. One wonders what the point is of the £27,000 system, other than preparing a generation for life in the database state and giving the school authorities the warm glow of control.

Once our privacy goes, we will lose it for ever

As I have said a few times before, once our privacy goes, we will lose it for ever. But try telling that to a popular press obsessed with crime, as well as scandal and celebrity, or the government. Both have an interest in stoking up fear, because fear sells newspapers, as well as repressive measures.

Think back 20 years and ask yourself if we would have accepted the almost casual announcement by the government that it planned to spy on all our private communications. It would have been out of the question because 20 years ago everyone knew what lay on the other side of the Iron Curtain. The same is true of the Transformational Government programme which will allow sharing of all our data horizontally as well as vertically, without our consent. The government will soon have what the Americans called 'total information awareness'. Nothing represents a greater threat to privacy.

A kind of panic exists in Britain which you do not find in other European countries. But ideology of sort is also at work. A paper by Perri 6, Charles Raab and Christine Bellamy, published in 2005, admitted a severe tension between data sharing and the right to privacy, which the government could not resolve. The

Blair administration first tried 'to find a way round data protection barriers', then resorted to the argument that guidelines and safeguards would protect the public from abuse and incompetence.

'It is a reflection of Labour's emphasis on rights and duties as reciprocal elements in citizens' relations with the state,' say the authors, 'that subjecting individuals' data to tests for risk is now regarded as the quid pro quo for their receiving help from public funds.'

Put in simple terms, the citizen is deemed to owe more to the state than ever before and in an era of anticipation - intelligence-led policing, early intervention in problem families and so forth - data sharing is essential for the authorities. What we should understand is that in this vast, bossy, communitarian project, a theft is taking place of a prized possession - privacy, the thing that once defined us.

When Andy Burnham, the Secretary of State for Culture, Media and Sport, said: 'The individual has no right to anonymity; the state has a right to know who you are', he unwittingly expressed the essence of Labour's programme.

The state has the right to know only a few details about us, but not who we are, just as it has no business monitoring our movements, communications and sharing our personal information with foreign powers. Or, for that matter, giving private companies access to 4.2 million profiles on the national DNA database, one million of which belong to innocent people.

Privacy law is being made in the courts piecemeal by judges responding to the supposed guarantees of the Human Rights Act. This is unsatisfactory. What we need is a new privacy law that takes in all these developments - not just the ones that appear before Justice Eady - and resolves the problems identified by Labour in its murmured deliberations about privacy and the database state. There are few more important issues that face this government or the next.

27 July 2008

Personal information toolkit

Information from the Information Commissioner's Office

What is personal information?

Personal information is information about you. It can be your name, address, or telephone number. It can also be the type of job you do, the things you buy when you are shopping and the place you went to school.

Why is managing my personal information important?

Today, like it or not, our personal information is held by many public and private organisations. These may include:

⇨ government departments.
⇨ banks and building societies gas, electric, phone and Internet service providers.
⇨ supermarkets and high-street retailers.
⇨ employers.
⇨ hospitals and doctors.
⇨ mail-order and Internet companies.
⇨ the police.
⇨ schools.
⇨ airlines and travel agents.
⇨ local councils.

What is my personal information used for?

Every day, you will give out your personal information in some way or other. It could be when you are shopping and you claim loyalty points, or in your workplace, or when you carry out a transaction with your bank.

But have you ever really thought about who you are giving your personal information to and what they will use it for?

Although most of the personal information stored about you will provide benefits like better medical care and financial reassurance, it also brings dangers. If your personal information is wrong, out of date or not held securely, it can cause problems. You could be unfairly refused a job, benefits or credit, or a place at college. In extreme cases, you could be a victim of identity theft or arrested for a crime you did not commit.

So what are my rights?

The Data Protection Act allows you to see information held about you and get it corrected if it is wrong. Organisations that hold your personal information must use it fairly, keep it secure, make sure the information is accurate and keep it up to date.

Every day, you will give out your personal information in some way or other

---

The Act also gives you the right to stop your personal information being used for unwanted marketing. The Privacy and Electronic Communications Regulations give you the right to stop electronic direct-marketing messages, including phone calls, faxes, emails and texts.

If you think an organisation may have breached the Data Protection Act in the way it holds and handles your personal information, you can complain to the Information Commissioner's Office.

For advice on how to complain, visit www.ico.gov.uk or telephone our helpline on 08456 306060.

Protecting your personal information

Your personal information is valuable, so you should treat it just as you would any valuable item.

With crimes like identity theft increasing, it is even more important for you to safeguard your information. Criminals can find out and use your personal details to open bank accounts, apply for credit cards and loans and get state benefits in your name.

Don't panic – there are some simple steps you can take to safeguard your information:

⇨ Store in a safe place any documents carrying your personal details, such as your passport, driving licence, bank statements and utility bills.
⇨ Shred or destroy personal documents you are throwing away

such as bills, receipts, bank or credit-card statements and other documents that show your name, address or other personal details.

⇨ If you have to post personal documents, ask the post office for advice on the most secure method.

⇨ Limit the number of documents you carry around that contain your personal details. If possible, don't leave personal documents in your vehicle.

⇨ Check your bank and credit-card statements regularly for unfamiliar transactions.

⇨ Use different passwords and PINs for different accounts and take extra care when using public computers to access your personal information.

⇨ Regularly get a copy of your personal credit file to check for any suspicious credit applications.

For more information on how to do this, see our website www.ico.gov.uk or ring 08453 091 091 for a free copy of 'Credit explained'.

⇨ Always think about who you are giving your information to. Be cautious about providing any personal details to unsolicited callers by phone, fax, post, email or in person, unless you are sure the person is who they say they are. If you are suspicious, ring the organisation back on an advertised number or visit their website.

⇨ Even if you know who is asking for your information, think twice before you answer their questions.

⇨ If it's not clear why they need the information, ask them or just move on to the next question.

⇨ Ensure your home computer is protected before you go online – buying a good anti-virus, firewall and anti-spam software package

will protect your computer against viruses and any spyware software, which can be used to obtain your personal information.

⇨ Do not click on links to go to a website unless you can be confident it is genuine.

⇨ If you use a central or communal postal-delivery point, such as in a block of flats, make sure you have a lockable postbox and collect your post as soon as possible. If your mail regularly fails to arrive, report this to Royal Mail.

⇨ If you move house, redirect all your mail and inform your bank, utility companies and other organisations of your new address.

⇨ The above information is reprinted with kind permission from the Information Commissioner's Office. Visit www.ico.gov.uk for more information.

© Information Commissioner's Office

Our surveillance society goes online

The potential for computers to read and understand data places our privacy under threat

By Christine Evans-Pughe

Being able to make your own decisions and hold your own views without interference; controlling information about yourself; and being in charge of your personal space – these basic elements of privacy are under threat, according to a new book, *The Spy in the Coffee Machine: The End of Privacy as We Know It*, by Kieron O'Hara and Nigel Shadbolt, two computer scientists at the University of Southampton.

While our offline activities are tracked by CCTV cameras, Oyster cards and RFID tags, the details of our online searches and purchases accumulate in databases that know more about us than we'd tell our closest friends. Many of us also broadcast our lives through blogs and social networking sites. 'When one's self as a social entity, with history, with transactions, is all out

there, then privacy is not the same old notion,' says Shadbolt, who is professor of artificial intelligence at Southampton and one of the leading scientists shaping the protocols for the future Internet.

As he and O'Hara point out, our attitude to privacy may stem from a lack of understanding that in the online world, the memory of an action will outlast the moment, and that the audience is much wider than your friends and family. Part of the reason for this complacency in the UK is that, historically, our data has never been misused by governments in terrible ways, says O'Hara. 'We're far more worried about being beaten up by drunken thugs on the street on a Friday night. We're also quite cynical,

and most of us have a sense, for instance, that CCTV data is probably completely useless 90% of the time.' (His assertion was confirmed this week when a senior policeman said that only 3% of street robberies are solved using CCTV.)

> **The details of our online searches and purchases accumulate in databases that know more about us than we'd tell our closest friends**

The end of privacy?

The authors' concerns are backed up by Privacy International's 2007 survey, which showed a worsening of privacy protection throughout the world. The UK fared badly, with the lowest privacy ranking in the EU – putting it in the 'endemic surveillance' category with Russia and Singapore.

The UK fared badly [in a 2007 survey], with the lowest privacy ranking in the EU – putting it in the 'endemic surveillance' category with Russia and Singapore

---

The power of computers makes it easy to share and amalgamate databases to reveal obscure information. Websites in the US use geographical information mashed with registers of convicted sex offenders to produce maps with markers locating the homes and crimes of any notified rapist or paedophile.

A couple of years ago, the hacker Tom Owad combined Amazon book wishlists with Google Earth data, filtering to leave only 'subversive' literature. The result: a world map of would-be readers of subversive books. Clicking on the location of the would-be reader would reveal a high-resolution satellite image of his or her house.

When the Internet goes fully semantic – and machines can read and understand all those scattered documents rather than just storing them – the potential for computers

to define us, undermine our privacy and demarcate our freedom of action will be even greater.

Shadbolt is chief technology officer of the digital identity startup Garlik, which is using such semantic search methods to give individuals more power over their information by offering a service for tracking sensitive personal data that can easily be found in the digital world. Garlik has also developed a rather engaging free measure of digital identity, QDOS. The QDOS algorithm looks at multiple presences of an individual on the web to produce a numerical score and a graphic illustration of how networked that person is, how digitally active and how much impact they have.

The potential, suggests Shadbolt, is for a new kind of digital psychometric. 'People have to be aware of their digital footprint,' he says. If you were rejected for a job on the basis of such an assessment, could you prove it? And what if your digital 'shape' showed something suspicious?

In the US, the Department of Homeland Security has been using similar techniques to visually display data patterns that show links between people, places and events. Last year, it had to suspend the activity, called ADVISE (Analysis, Dissemination, Visualisation, Insight and Semantic Enhancement) on the grounds that it violated federal privacy standards.

Nothing to fear?

Her Majesty's Revenue and Customs (HMRC) did us all a favour, in the authors' view, by last year losing two discs containing all of the child benefit database. With half the

UK population left contemplating how criminals might use such data to plunder bank accounts or steal identities, it became clear that the 'nothing to hide, nothing to fear' line used to reassure us about the merits of the database state doesn't stand up.

Shadbolt says the risks of data spillage are greater than we're led to believe: 'If you keep within the law, and the government keeps within the law, and its employees keep within the law, and the computer holding the database doesn't screw up, and the system is carefully designed according to well-understood software engineering principles and maintained properly, and the government doesn't scrimp on the outlay and all the data are entered carefully and the police are adequately trained to use the system and the system isn't hacked into, and your identity isn't stolen, and the local hardware functions, well, you have nothing to fear.'

But Shadbolt and O'Hara explain 19th-century philosopher John Stuart Mill's view that society was capable of applying so much pressure that citizens might be prevented from making sensible or moral choices. Privacy is associated with the autonomy that Mill felt we needed because it enables us to make choices freely. If we value this freedom, say the authors, we will all have to play a much more active role in keeping privacy in place.

⇨ *The Spy in the Coffee Machine: The End of Privacy as We Know It* by Kieron O'Hara and Nigel Shadbolt (Oneworld Publications, £9.99)
8 May 2008

Social networking and privacy

PCC research: public concern about social networking and privacy

Forty-two per cent of web users aged 16-24 know someone who has been embarrassed by information uploaded on to the Internet without their consent. And 78% of the entire adult online population would change information they publish about themselves online if they thought the material would later be reproduced in the mainstream media.

Forty-two per cent of web users aged 16-24 know someone who has been embarrassed by information uploaded on to the Internet without their consent

---

These are among the findings of new research into public attitudes to social networking, commissioned from Ipsos MORI by the Press Complaints Commission. It reveals the huge popularity of social networking sites in the UK today – used by 83% of 16- to 24-year-olds who go online and half the total population of adult web users. Yet, only just over half of users (55%) think before posting information that it might later be used by third parties without their consent.

Public concern is demonstrated by the fact that 89% of web users think there should be clear guidelines about the type of personal information that can be published online so that they can complain if this material is wrong or intrusive.

The PCC will be holding an event in conjunction with the Westminster Media Forum at the Royal Over-Seas League on Thursday, 5 June, at which representatives of the media, legal, online and political worlds will discuss these issues further.

Commenting on the findings and the Westminster Forum Event, PCC Chairman Sir Christopher Meyer said:

'Social networking marks a huge cultural change in the way in which people communicate. Personal information is being put into the public domain on an unprecedented scale. There is a need for public awareness about what can happen to information once it is voluntarily put into the public domain.

'This clearly has implications for the PCC, which has always had the task of deciding where to draw the boundaries between what newspapers and magazines may legitimately publish and what can rightly be considered private. The challenge remains the same for online editorial content, including material taken from social networking sites. In the digital age, self-regulation, with its sound principles and speed of operation, has never been more relevant. That is why I expect our current Code of Practice to be able to handle complaints in this area; and in the process to enable the Commission over the coming months and years to define through its decisions the boundary between the private and the public.

'But there are wider cultural and other issues going beyond the PCC to be debated, which is why we have taken the initiative of conducting the survey and holding today's event at the Westminster Media Forum.'

Note

1 1,000 GB web users aged 16-64 were interviewed by Ipsos MORI between 14 and 18 March 2008. Participants were recruited via an online panel and the sample is representative of the GB online population.

5 June 2008

⇨ The above information is re-printed with kind permission from the Press Complaints Commission. Visit www.pcc.org.uk for more information.

Facebook and the death of privacy

In order for public and private life to thrive, we need spaces that are absolutely free from the prying eyes of officialdom and others

By Rob Killick

New developments in social networking, like Facebook and MySpace, encourage a blurring of the private and public, while a range of Internet service providers track our online behaviour. In the UK, our every movement and action seems to be subject to state surveillance, including areas of our lives that we normally assume to be private and confidential. Those who value anonymity have good reason to be concerned. How can we balance our privacy with the desire to take advantage of these new web resources?

Facebook, the social networking phenomenon, has often come under fire for the way it gathers and claims ownership of masses of personal information that users submit to it. It is currently being investigated by the UK Information Commissioner's Office (ICO) after a user complained about not being able to delete their profile, even after terminating an account.

Like most Facebook subscribers, this disgruntled person might have failed to read the terms and conditions for sign-up. These clearly state that Facebook owns all the data users add to the site: 'By posting Member Content to any part of the website, you automatically grant, and you represent and warrant that you have the right to grant, to Facebook an irrevocable, perpetual, non-exclusive, transferable, fully paid, worldwide license to use, copy, perform, display, reformat, translate, excerpt and distribute such information and content and to prepare derivative works of, or incorporate into other works, such information and content, and to grant and authorise sublicenses of the foregoing...'

While social networking sites such as Facebook and MySpace effectively own the data we post on their sites, Internet companies like Google and Yahoo keep records of what we look for on their search engines. Google co-founder Eric Schmidt's ambition is to be able to gather enough information about us that we will be able to seek answers from the search engine even on such personal questions as 'What shall I do tomorrow?' and 'What job shall I take?'

Our telephone call records are available to up to 800 state bodies under the RIP Act

Essentially, what these companies do with this information is up to them – and this is already leading to some iniquities. In November 2007, Jerry Yang, CEO of Yahoo, was called a 'moral pygmy' at the US Foreign Affairs Committee for handing over the identities of Chinese dissidents to the Chinese government, resulting in one dissident being sentenced to 10 years in jail.

Privacy and state surveillance

It would be hard to disagree with this judgement of Yang, but we should also remember that the US government itself has the power to subpoena similar information from any search engine business. In the UK, Internet Service Providers (ISPs) are asked to maintain a reasonable intercept capability under the Regulation of Investigatory Powers (RIP) Act so that the security services can track suspects' use of email and the websites they visit.

Add the fact that, when we're offline, CCTV tracks our movements, our telephone call records are available to up to 800 state bodies under the RIP Act, and that our credit card and banking records are similarly obtainable, and it becomes clear that we all leave behind us an electronic trail which can be reconstituted into a detailed record of our lives. It is hard to see what remains private these days beyond face-to-face conversations with friends and loved ones.

But is this really a cause for concern? Some would argue that concern with such data tracking and retention is paranoid and alarmist. The government would argue that having the power to view our personal data will help catch potential terrorists or criminals. And, from the point of view of convenient consumption, if Google can ensure that we receive only targeted marketing rather than torrents of useless information and spam emails, then isn't personalisation to the benefit of us all?

Cyberspace is not a private space

It was always a utopian belief that cyberspace could become a zone of freedom in an otherwise regulated world. The net has, if anything, become an even less private space than the real world. In his perceptive 1999 book, *Code and Other Laws of Cyberspace*, American lawyer Lawrence Lessig wrote: 'When we see the path that cyberspace is on we see that much of the "liberty" present at cyberspace's founding will vanish in its future. Values that we now consider fundamental will not necessarily remain. Freedoms that were fundamental will slowly disappear.'

The problem is that it is not just the illusory freedom that cyberspace offered in the early, heady days which is disappearing as we move more and more of our activities online. Take the web 'browser', for instance. Traditionally, browsing is what you do in a library or a shop. It is essentially a private act. It is up to you what books you pick up, read, take notes from, etc. It is a personal experience and it leaves no trace. Web browsing on the other hand has no privacy inherent in it at all. Law enforcement agencies or marketers can find out exactly what online material you have accessed, how long you spent on each page and how many times you have visited the same websites.

There are many great examples of how the Internet has allowed us to transform the way we share and use knowledge, including the excellent initiatives of world-renowned institutions such as the Bodleian Library to put their entire collections online. But this also means that which books we access, when and for how long will be recorded for ever.

While there are good reasons to be enthusiastic about new forms of communication and information sharing, we increasingly find that we have to sacrifice our privacy in the process. Contrary to Facebook's all-out ownership claims, the principle of informed consent should be at the centre of digital tracking. Websites and search engines should offer a 'no tracking' button, which means that the record of which sites we look at is automatically deleted unless you give express permission for it to be kept. In other words, there should be an opt-in rather than an opt-out.

Privacy, publishing and public life

There is some added confusion around the privacy issue now because of the apparent willingness of many, especially young people, to record on blogs and social network sites minute and often embarrassing, even incriminating, details of their lives. Some of this activity, as others have noted, represents an attempt to connect in a fragmented social world. Some of it is also a matter of youthful naivety, which as the longer-term consequences of recording private details online become clear, will

probably be tempered. Some of it is down to people simply not giving a toss – a prerogative of youth.

The fact that people choose to put private information on the web which can later compromise them in some way is not, to my mind, principally a privacy issue. Choosing to put information into the public domain remains what it always has been, even prior to the Internet: a form of publishing. This really is a case of 'publish and be damned', a principle that also applies to emails and any other form of communication. There is no such thing as a 'private email', just as there was never such thing as a 'private letter'. Once sent off, what happens to the content is up to the recipient. What we write and say always has consequences and learning this lesson is simply part of growing up.

The problem arises if we cannot share anything at all in private with other people, if everything we do is potentially intruded on by outsiders. For some people, the need for privacy is important in itself and that is fair enough. It is one of the most profound problems of the surveillance society that the anonymity of urban life has been diminished. In this sense, it does not matter if anybody, whether it's an individual, the state or an Internet company, actually intends to harm us by collecting our private data. The sheer weight of data available on us now is itself oppressive, rendering us completely visible whether we like it or not. Our awareness of this must be influencing the way most of us think, feel and act in ways that we are perhaps not yet entirely clear about.

There is one area in which this lack of privacy is having an obvious effect. The difficulty of keeping part of yourself private has a deep impact on someone's ability to play a role as a public figure. Anybody considering a role in public life these days has to be prepared for exposure of their private lives in a way that would not have been true in the past. Given the ordinary fallibilities of human beings there can be few people who can confidently put themselves forward for public scrutiny. This does not mean that the same people would not have much to offer as public figures. There have been many exceptional leaders in politics, business and the arts in the past who would not have stood the modern celebrity culture exposing of their private activities.

There are as yet no clear lines about what level of online data surveillance, retention or use is acceptable in a democracy. But one thing is certain: it is only through contesting the right of any state or private body to observe and record our actions that a proper debate can take place on what should or should not be permitted in this area. Insisting on transparency of who is retaining what information on whom is an important step in this process. A good place to start for us as individuals would be to ask where the opt-in button is.

Rob Killick is CEO of cScape.
7 February 2008

⇨ The above information is reprinted with kind permission from Spiked. Visit www.spiked-online.com for more information.

UK consumers wake up to privacy

Information from the Information Commissioner's Office

Eight out of ten of us now take greater care in the way we look after our personal information, according to new research published today by the privacy watchdog, the Information Commissioner's Office (ICO).

The nationwide survey suggests recent high profile data losses have had a significant impact on the way we now manage our personal information. Eighty-eight per cent of us have started checking our bank statements on a more regular basis and 85% now refuse to give out personal details wherever possible.

Three-quarters of us now worry more about the safety of our personal information than ever before

---

The figures show that three-quarters of us now worry more about the safety of our personal information than ever before. Fifty-three per cent say we no longer have confidence in the way organisations such as banks, local authorities and government departments handle our personal information.

David Smith, Deputy Commissioner at the ICO, said: 'I encourage everyone to check how organisations are storing their personal details. You can use your rights under the Data Protection Act to ensure your data is being properly looked after – use our checklist to ask the right questions. Taking care of our personal information has never been so important and, as the research shows, the majority of us are now much more aware of the value of our personal details. As more and more personal information is collected, the risk grows that some information will be inaccurate, out of date or end up in the wrong hands.'

According to the research seven out of ten individuals feel powerless about how their personal information is looked after. The ICO is today urging individuals to use rights under the Data Protection Act in order to regain some control over their personal information. The ICO has published a user-friendly guide to data protection rights which includes a data protection checklist. The checklist outlines the questions which we should ask before giving out our details in order to 'check' an organisation's data protection practices.

David Smith said: 'For any of us to have trust in an organisation we must be confident that our information is held securely and processed in line with data protection rules. If we all regularly start to ask the right questions then organisations will respond to public demand and take the protection of our personal information more seriously. If organisations fail to recognise the importance of data protection they not only risk losing business. They could also face action from the ICO.'

19 March 2008

⇨ The above information is reprinted with kind permission from the Information Commissioner's Office. Visit www.ico.gov.uk for more information.

© *Information Commissioner's Office*

Monitoring at work

What rights do you have if you think your boss is secretly checking up on you?

Whether you like it or not, employers have the right to monitor your activities at work in many ways. For example they can:

⇨ Use CCTV cameras;
⇨ Open your work mail;
⇨ Open your email or check it with automated software;
⇨ Check phone logs or record phone calls;
⇨ Check your web browsing history;
⇨ Get information about you from credit reference agencies;
⇨ Monitor performance through tills and checkouts.

There are some safeguards, primarily that:

⇨ The monitoring must relate to the business;
⇨ The equipment being monitored must be provided partly or wholly for work;
⇨ Your employer must have made all reasonable efforts to inform you that your communications will be monitored.

But in practice these don't restrain an employer very much. Monitoring can be used without your consent in many circumstances, including:

⇨ To establish facts which are relevant to the business, to check that procedures are being followed, or to check standards, for example, listening in to phone-calls to assess the quality of your work;
⇨ To prevent or detect crime;
⇨ To check for unauthorised use of equipment – e.g. using the Internet or email for personal use;
⇨ To make sure electronic systems are operating effectively, for example, to prevent computer viruses entering the system;
⇨ To check whether an email or phone-call is relevant to the business. In this case, your employer can open up your emails or listen to voice-mails but is not allowed to record your calls;

By Tom Green

⇨ To check incoming calls if you work on a confidential help line. In this case, your employer can listen in, but is not allowed to record these calls;
⇨ In the interests of national security.

So, basically, don't expect much privacy when you're online or on the phone at work.

Spy boss

Secret monitoring, however, for example by hidden cameras or audio recorders, is very rarely legal. Guidance under data protection law says that secret monitoring should not be allowed in private areas at work, such as staff toilets, unless there is serious crime involved, such as drug dealing.

Policies

Ideally, an employer should have a code of conduct or policy that covers workplace monitoring. If a code or policy has been agreed, it will usually form part of your contract of employment. This means that where an employer is allowed to monitor your activities, these activities could be the subject of disciplinary action if you are using workplace equipment in ways that are not permitted in your contract of employment. The employment relations organisation Acas has produced a short guide on Internet and email policies that gives some insight into the employer's point of view.

Drugs

The legal position for drug testing at work is complicated but it's acknowledged that employers have a justifiable interest in employees' drug use in certain circumstances. These include employees using drugs or alcohol in the workplace, or if drug or alcohol use is affecting your

performance or safety at work. But a drug test shouldn't be imposed on you, and should only be introduced after a consultation.

Complaints

If you're unhappy with the way you are being monitored at work, and can't resolve it with your employer, you can call the office of the Information Commissioner on 01625 545 745.

Thanks to the CAB for help with this article.

⇨ The above information is reprinted with kind permission from TheSite. Visit www.thesite.org for more information.

© TheSite

Identity theft

Frequently asked questions

What is identity crime?

Identity crime is a generic term for identity theft, creating a false identity or committing identity fraud.

What does identity theft cost the UK?

The 2002 Cabinet Office Study, which covered the use of false identities and the theft of other people's identities, estimated that crime facilitated by identity fraud costs the UK economy £1.3 billion per annum.

Criminals commit identity theft by stealing your personal information and then pretending to be you

---

In February 2006, the Home Office Identity Fraud Steering Committee completed a one-off exercise to update the Cabinet Office estimate for the purpose of establishing trends in the intervening years. This exercise estimated that identity fraud costs the UK economy £1.7 billion a year. As with the previous study, it represented a best estimate of the scale of the problem.

The Identity Fraud Steering Committee developed a new methodology for estimating the cost of identity fraud, and together with key industry stakeholders, published a new estimate of £1.2 billion on 9 October 2008.

What is being done about identity theft in the UK?

The Home Office, in collaboration with other government departments and private sector organisations, set up the Home Office Identity Fraud Steering Committee to lead a cross public/private sector work programme to tackle identity theft and identity fraud.

How does a criminal get my personal information?

Criminals commit identity theft by stealing your personal information and then pretending to be you. This is often done by taking documents from your rubbish or by making contact with you and pretending to be from a legitimate organisation.

What does a criminal do with my personal information?

Once a criminal has the information he needs he could for example:

⇨ apply for a credit card in your name;
⇨ open a bank or building society account in your name;
⇨ apply for other financial services in your name;
⇨ run up debts (e.g. use your credit/debit card details to make purchase) or obtain a loan in your name;
⇨ apply for any benefits in your name (e.g. housing benefit, new tax credits, income support, jobseeker's allowance, child benefit);
⇨ apply for a driving licence in your name;
⇨ register a vehicle in your name;
⇨ apply for a passport in your name; or
⇨ apply for a mobile phone contract in your name.

If I'm a victim, am I responsible for any fraudulent credit card or bank transactions?

If you have been a victim of identity fraud and your card is still in your possession, you should not have to pay for anything bought on it without your permission (subject to the terms and conditions of your account). If your card has been lost or stolen, you will usually not have to pay, unless it can be shown that you have acted fraudulently or without reasonable care, for example by keeping your PIN number written down with your card. The same applies to any money lost through fraudulent bank transactions.

How can I tell if I'm a victim of identity theft?

You may become a victim of identity theft if:

⇨ you have lost or had stolen important documents such as your passport or driving licence; or
⇨ post expected from your bank has not arrived or you are receiving no post at all.

You may already be a victim of identity theft if:

⇨ items have appeared on your bank or credit card statements that you do not recognise;
⇨ you applied for a state benefit but are told that you are already claiming;
⇨ you receive bills, invoices or receipts addressed to you for goods or services you haven't asked for;
⇨ you have been refused a financial service, such as a credit card or a loan, despite having a good credit history;
⇨ a mobile phone contract has been set up in your name without your knowledge; or
⇨ you have received letters from solicitors or debt collectors for debts that aren't yours.

⇨ The above information is reprinted with kind permission from Identity Theft. Visit www.identity-theft.org.uk for more information.

© *Identity Theft*

⇨ Privacy is recognised around the world in diverse regions and cultures. It is protected in the Universal Declaration of Human Rights, the International Covenant on Civil and Political Rights, and in many other international and regional human rights treaties. Nearly every country in the world includes a right of privacy in its constitution. (page 1)

⇨ The recognition of privacy is deeply rooted in history. There is recognition of privacy in the Qur'an and in the sayings of Muhammad. The Bible has numerous references to privacy. Jewish law has long recognised the concept of being free from being watched. There were also protections in classical Greece and ancient China. (page 2)

⇨ Article 12 of the 1948 Universal Declaration of Human Rights states: 'No one should be subjected to arbitrary interference with his privacy, family, home or correspondence, nor to attacks on his honour or reputation. Everyone has the right to the protection of the law against such interferences or attacks.' (page 3)

⇨ Britain has more closed circuit TV cameras (CCTV) than any other country, monitoring streets, stations, shopping centres, offices etc. 74% of people surveyed felt this was broadly a good thing, as CCTV cameras help to deter criminal behaviour and catch offenders. (page 5)

⇨ The right to respect for privacy became enforceable in UK courts as recently as October 2000 via the Human Rights Act 1998. (page 6)

⇨ The UK is the world leader in CCTV use with approximately 4.2 million cameras in operation. (page 7)

⇨ With an estimated 3.9 million samples, the national DNA database is five times larger than any other national database and contains samples taken from many who have never been convicted of any offence. (page 7)

⇨ Every day the average person makes three mobile phone calls and sends at least two text messages. Each time the network provider logs information about who was called as well as the caller's location and direction of travel, worked out by triangulation from phone masts. (page 8)

⇨ 43% of people surveyed held the view that DNA data should be held only for convicted criminals, and data on everyone else's DNA destroyed. 51% held the view that in order to catch more criminals, the police should be able to build up their DNA database, so that eventually they hold DNA data on every citizen. (page 11)

⇨ Nearly a million innocent people could have their records removed from the national DNA database after a court ruled holding them breached their human rights. (page 12)

⇨ Two-thirds of councils have taken up the snooping powers open to them under the Regulation of Investigative Powers Act since its introduction in 2000. (page 20)

⇨ Under RIPA, councils can conduct surveillance if they suspect criminal activity; they can also ask for subscriber details of Internet and telephone bills but they cannot tap phones or intercept emails. (page 21)

⇨ CCTV involves the use of an unmanned, remotely mounted video camera system, transmitting live pictures back to a television screen where developments can be monitored and recorded. (page 22)

⇨ The use of commercial satellite imagery by governments has increased substantially in recent years. (page 26)

⇨ The latest figures available show that under current laws, 500,000 requests were made during one year for private communications data. That figure is up on the previous two years by almost 30 per cent. (page 30)

⇨ Every day, you will give out your personal information in some way or other. It could be when you are shopping and you claim loyalty points, or in your workplace, or when you carry out a transaction with your bank. (page 31)

⇨ A senior policeman has claimed that only 3% of street robberies are solved using CCTV. (page 32)

⇨ Forty-two per cent of web users aged 16-24 know someone who has been embarrassed by information uploaded on to the Internet without their consent. And 78 per cent of the entire adult online population would change information they publish about themselves online if they thought the material would later be reproduced in the mainstream media. (page 34)

⇨ Our telephone call records are available to up to 800 state bodies under the RIP Act. (page 35)

⇨ Eight out of ten of us now take greater care in the way we look after our personal information, according to new research published by the privacy watchdog, the Information Commissioner's Office (ICO). (page 37)

⇨ The 2002 Cabinet Office Study, which covered the use of false identities and the theft of other people's identities, estimated that crime facilitated by identity fraud costs the UK economy £1.3 billion per annum. (page 39)

GLOSSARY

Big Brother

Big Brother is a figure in the novel 'Nineteen Eighty-Four', George Orwell's story of a future totalitarian Britain in which citizens are constantly monitored and their behaviour controlled. Big Brother, a moustached man representing the novel's totalitarian government, appears on posters designed to intimidate citizens accompanied by the slogan 'Big Brother is watching you'. The phrase 'Big Brother' is therefore often used by the media as an analogy for a condition of total and constant surveillance. *Big Brother* is also the title of a television reality show in which contestants are constantly monitored by hidden cameras and their actions broadcast to the public.

Biometric data

Biometric data is unique to each individual. Examples of biometric data would include a fingerprint, iris recognition and a photograph. Travel documents issued by the UK Border Agency since 17 March 2008 now include biometric data in a chip which acts as a unique identifier. It is likely that the government's planned ID cards will also include biometric data.

CCTV

Closed circuit television. These are mounted cameras which broadcast a live image to a television screen, which can then be monitored and recorded. They are used primarily for security purposes. With an estimated 4.2 million cameras in operation, the UK has more CCTV monitoring than any other country.

Data Protection Act 1998

This act allows you to see information that is held about you by organisations of all types, such as the NHS in the public sector or your bank in the private sector. Examples of personal information include your name, address and telephone number, your bank account number, your medical records and the things you buy when you are shopping.

DNA

Deoxyribonucleic acid. DNA is an acid containing genetic instructions which are unique to each individual. Genetic material such as hair, when discovered at a crime scene, can be used to identify the perpetrator of the crime if police have another sample of his/her DNA against which to compare it. This is why the UK has a national DNA database, containing an estimated 3.9 million DNA samples. The database is controversial, however, as some of the samples have been taken from individuals who have never been convicted of any offence. A recent EU ruling judged that keeping an innocent person's DNA on record is in breach of their human right to privacy.

Freedom of Information Act 2000

This act gives you the right to see official information held by public authorities such as local councils, hospitals and the police. For example, you could ask your local council for information about hygiene inspections in local restaurants or ask a university for exam pass rates.

Identity theft

When a criminal is able to gain possession of an individual's personal information, they can then masquerade as that person. Under their stolen identity, they may be able to make purchases using your bank account or gain credit using your identity, or apply for jobs in your name.

National Identity Scheme

This refers to the government's plan to issue ID cards to the UK population. The cards will not be compulsory. They will carry personal data about the holder, including biometric data, and the government claim the cards will help combat identity theft, offer a convenient way to prove one's age and make travel easier. However, critics fear that the cards will enable the government to collect and store large amounts of personal data on UK citizens, further encroaching on our personal privacy and with the potential to be misused by unscrupulous individuals who may be able to gain access.

Privacy

There is no single definition of privacy, and descriptions vary widely according to context and environment. In terms of UK law, however, privacy may be said to refer to the individual's right to control their personal information and live their life free of unjustifiable intrusion or surveillance.

RIPA

The Regulation of Investigatory Powers Act. This was introduced in 2000 and gives certain authorities the right to intercept communications and use other surveillance methods where there is suspicion of a crime being committed. The measures were designed to help combat terrorism; however, the Act became the subject of controversy when it was revealed that some local councils were using the new powers for petty 'snooping'.

Surveillance

Literally, to be watched. The UK has been described by some as a 'surveillance society' due in part to factors including its large number of CCTV cameras, national DNA database and planned identity card scheme.

Universal Declaration of Human Rights

This 1948 document, drawn up after the Second World War as a response to the horrors of the Holocaust, enshrines the right to privacy in Article 12.

INDEX

Additional Resources

Other Issues titles

If you are interested in researching further some of the issues raised in *Privacy and Surveillance*, you may like to read the following titles in the **Issues** series:

⇨ Vol. 167 *Our Human Rights* (ISBN 978 1 86168 471 4)

⇨ Vol. 158 *The Internet Revolution* (ISBN 978 1 86168 451 6)

⇨ Vol. 147 *The Terrorism Problem* (ISBN 978 1 86168 420 2)

⇨ Vol. 142 *Media Issues* (ISBN 978 1 86168 408 0)

⇨ Vol. 137 *Crime and Anti-Social Behaviour* (ISBN 978 1 86168 389 2)

⇨ Vol. 134 *Customers and Consumerism* (ISBN 978 1 86168 386 1)

⇨ Vol. 121 *The Censorship Debate* (ISBN 978 1 86168 354 0)

For more information about these titles, visit our website at www.independence.co.uk/publicationslist

Useful organisations

You may find the websites of the following organisations useful for further research:

⇨ **Home Office:** www.homeoffice.gov.uk

⇨ **Identity and Passport Service:** www.ips.gov.uk

⇨ **Info4Security:** www.info4security.com

⇨ **Information Commissioner's Office:** www.ico.gov.uk

⇨ **Liberty:** www.liberty-human-rights.org.uk

⇨ **Local Government Association:** www.lga.gov.uk

⇨ **NO2ID Campaign:** www.no2id.net

⇨ **Politics.co.uk:** www.politics.co.uk

⇨ **Press Complaints Commission:** www.pcc.org.uk

⇨ **Privacy International:** www.privacyinternational.org

⇨ **RINF:** http://rinf.com

⇨ **Statewatch:** www.statewatch.org

⇨ **UK Border Agency:** http://ukba.homeoffice.gov.uk

ACKNOWLEDGEMENTS

The publisher is grateful for permission to reproduce the following material.

While every care has been taken to trace and acknowledge copyright, the publisher tenders its apology for any accidental infringement or where copyright has proved untraceable. The publisher would be pleased to come to a suitable arrangement in any such case with the rightful owner.

Chapter One: A Surveillance Society?

Overview of privacy, © Privacy International, *A Surveillance Society?*, © Info4Security, *Overlooked*, © Liberty, *How Big Brother watches your every move*, © Telegraph Group Limited, *Surveillance in the EU*, © Statewatch, *Checks on surveillance*, © Crown copyright is reproduced with the permission of Her Majesty's Stationery Office, *Freedom of information and data protection*, © Information Commissioner's Office, *The national DNA database*, © Crown copyright is reproduced with the permission of Her Majesty's Stationery Office, *Britons win DNA landmark decision*, © MSN, *Biometric travel documents*, © Crown copyright is reproduced with the permission of Her Majesty's Stationery Office, *A step too far?*, © Information Commissioner's Office, *Benefits of the National Identity Scheme*, © Crown copyright is reproduced with the permission of Her Majesty's Stationery Office, *Public opinion on ID cards*, © The NO2ID campaign, *ID card myths*, © Crown copyright is reproduced with the permission of Her Majesty's Stationery Office, *The problems with ID cards*, © The NO2ID campaign, *Councils ordered to stop snooping on residents*, © RINF, *How councils are using surveillance*, © Press Association, *Council leaders respond to 'snooping' allegations*, © Local Government Association, *CCTV*, © Adfero, *CCTV and crime prevention*, © The Scotsman, *Predicting crime with CCTV*, © Net Communities, *CCTV and sound recording*, © Out-law.com, *CCTV in schools*, © ATL, *Satellite surveillance*, © Privacy International, *Privacy and the media*, © Liberty, *Mosley's victory has a hollow ring for the rest of us*, © Guardian Newspapers Limited.

Chapter Two: Personal Privacy Issues

Personal information toolkit, © Information Commissioner's Office, *Our surveillance society goes online*, © Guardian Newspapers Limited, *Social networking and privacy*, © Press Complaints Commission, *Facebook and the death of privacy*, © Spiked, *UK consumers wake up to privacy*, © Information Commissioner's Office, *Monitoring at work*, © TheSite, *Identity theft*, © Identity Theft.

Photographs

Flickr: pages 20 (Daniel); 25 (Jim Sher). **Stock Xchng:** pages 8 (Brano Hudak); 12 (Craig Jewell); 13, 23 (Steve Woods); 15 (Florian Rieder); 16 (Sophie); 22 (Chris Cockram); 27 (Helen Lee); 39 (Lotus Head). **Wikimedia Commons:** page 2 (public domain).

Illustrations

Pages 1, 18, 31, 33: Simon Kneebone; pages 4, 34, 37: Angelo Madrid; pages 6, 26, 36, 38: Don Hatcher; pages 12, 28: Bev Aisbett.

Additional editorial by Claire Owen, on behalf of Independence Educational Publishers.

And with thanks to the team: Mary Chapman, Sandra Dennis, Claire Owen and Jan Sunderland.

Lisa Firth
Cambridge
January, 2009